*Have you eve... ....
before?" Has someone phoned you
just as you thought of them? Ever
experience a series of uncanny
"coincidences," or hit it off with a
person you just "knew" you'd like?*

If you've ever had any of these things happen
to you, you've had a psychic experience. Let
Robert A. Ferguson show you how to develop,
in a planned and simple way, that innate, un-
tapped psychic power with *ESP For Everyone*.
Using a commonsense—not a theoretical—approach, it's filled with case histories, individual exercises, group activities to share with
friends, and a glossary of psychic terms.

Enlightening and fun, *ESP For Everyone*
is about learning to use your intuition to build
the happy, prosperous, successful life you
want to live. Start today!

ESP
FOR
EVERYONE

ROBERT A. FERGUSON

ST. MARTIN'S PRESS / NEW YORK

ESP FOR EVERYONE

Copyright © 1989 by Robert A. Ferguson.

ISBN: 0-312-91179-3   Can. ISBN: 0-312-91178-5

Printed in the United States of America

First St. Martin's Press mass market edition/February 1989

10 9 8 7 6 5 4 3 2 1

This book is dedicated
to my editor,
Peter St. John Ginna

And my heartfelt thanks to artist Carol L. Johnson, of San
Jose, for the drawings found in this book.

CONTENTS

vii

PART THREE

FOREWORD

There's nothing wrong with wanting a happier, more successful, and prosperous life. The will to achieve, the urge to want more, is a natural part of the human personality. To progress, one must use every talent available to reach personal goals, but there is one talent that is rarely used. That talent is ESP, and it can make the difference between success and failure. Most important, it's something you can learn to use for your personal enrichment.

For over twenty years I've taught psychic development classes based upon the same material you'll be using in this book. And my program works! I've taught people from every walk of life and from almost every profession. Each person attended the classes for his or her own personal reasons, but with one common goal: to get the extra help we all need to achieve what we want.

I am often asked, "When did you become aware that you were psychic?" That's a question I can't answer because I can't remember when I was other than I am right now. My parents and older members of the family have said that everyone knew I was "different" by the time I was old enough to walk, so take their word for it. I do remember clearly that there was always some family member taking me to psychic demonstrations, séances, astrologers, and all those other strange places where I met such strange people. I loved it. In one way or another I've always been connected with the psychic world, though often in changing roles.

I'm a person who values his privacy and lives fairly simply. High visibility and name recognition are antithetical to that way of life. I was never able to balance the two. I went through the "Hollywood scene" and met some very fine people. But the mere fact that I was associated with some very famous people gave me more publicity than I wanted. Then, I'd have to withdraw from the public eye for a while.

I cannot remember a time when there weren't people asking me how they could learn to be psychic. For years my answer was, "I don't know," but in fact I did know. I was just too lazy to put any real thought into it. Still, all along, I felt an "inner urging" that finally became so strong I felt I had no choice but to develop a method to teach others to recognize the psychic ability they already had. It took some time to iron out the wrinkles. At last, I came up with a successful method and have been teaching by that method ever since. But I have also always kept an open mind, ready to accept or reject past or present views.

I feel a great deal of excitement about the research being done on the right brain/left brain theories. Most psychics have always known about that schism, only we used different terminology than the scientists. We refer to the conscious/subconscious mind, or to the male/female part of the brain. There remains no question in my mind that before too much time has passed, science will produce the evidence to support what I will teach you in this book.

Practical Uses of ESP

There is no limit to the practical uses of ESP. I've given a few examples below, but as you begin the study program, you'll realize the truth of my assertion. It simply becomes another extension of your personality.

In the past, many of my classes have been conducted for groups from the same profession—the majority of which have been from the field of law enforcement. For these men and women, the emphasis was placed upon "feeling danger" and teaching them how to see the human aura so they could know the personality of the person being dealt with and answer such questions as, were they dangerous? I've had a great deal of feedback from these groups, and their comments have all been positive. "Feeling danger" before the danger presented itself is a crucial ability for anyone who needs to be prepared and to protect themselves and others.

Many accountants have also attended my classes. ESP helps them to avoid errors or to find the error quickly so it can be corrected.

Physicians who have attended my classes have done so because they needed more help in diagnosing and treating patients. The importance of early detection is obviously of great importance in the practice of medicine, and ESP has helped many a physician to find a problem before the appearance of its first physical symptoms.

Being a parent is not easy. I believe that *ESP for Everyone* will be invaluable to the parent. Besides telling you when danger confronts your child, ESP helps you to see the hidden talents of a youngster. When you know in what area the "genetic dice" have given the child a head start, you can create the environment that will nurture those strengths.

There isn't anything weird or supernatural about

extrasensory perception. ESP is a modern synonym for the more familiar words *intuition* or *instinct*. And that is what *ESP for Everyone* is all about—learning to use intuition, or instinct, to build a better future, the life you want to live, the way you want to live it.

Mythology tells of a conference of the gods at the creation of the universe.

One god said, "Let's give man the same power of creation that we possess."

"Where shall we conceal this priceless gift?" another asked.

A third god replied, "Let's hide the gift where man will never think to look for it—within his own mind."

ESP for Everyone is a guide that shows you how to unlock the treasure of your own mind. This book is written as an appeal to your common sense. It will teach you a practical, step-by-step method for using the intuitive treasure that's buried within your subconscious mind. I will explain what psychic abilities you do possess and how to use them.

ESP for Everyone consists of an eight-week development program that explains in a practical, not theoretical, manner how to become a more successful you. It's a commonsense approach to happier living. You will *use* your psychic talents, not just think about them. And it's fun! No previous experience necessary, though you've undoubtedly had a great deal more experience than you presently realize.

Ever had a hunch? Believe in women's intuition? Ever had a dream come true? Has anyone ever called you on the telephone just as you were thinking of them? If any of these things have happened to you, you've had a psychic experience.

Whatever your occupation, your hobby, your desires, this book can help make your goals attainable, your dreams come true.

PART

I

INTRODUCTION

At the moment, you're probably unaware of all the mental obstacles that stand in the way of your psychic development. You may be wondering whether this type of personal growth is valid, false, good, or bad. That these questions arise is not surprising. There has been so much erroneous information perpetuated by a vocal few that it's often difficult for the uninitiated not to ask such questions.

The "book burners," as I call them, have determined that the pursuit of psychic knowledge in any form is, in the least, eccentric, at the most, the work of the devil. These extremes do not stand the test of common sense. They have created an environment in which the subconscious mind can build a psychological tomb in which to bury the creative psychic mind.

This introduction to *ESP for Everyone* is included as a tool to help free your mind of the many mental obstacles that have subconsciously influenced the exercise of your inherent psychic power. An open mind and a positive attitude can help to fulfill the promise of a happy, successful, and prosperous life.

There are many questions concerning the psychic world that must be addressed before beginning the psychic lessons that follow.

My first endeavor will be to explain what your psychic powers really are, how they function, and how they can be put to work in a beneficial, nondestructive manner. I will attempt to remove any doubts you might harbor regarding the ethical or moral nature of personal psychic development.

What Is Being Psychic?

Being psychic simply means that an individual consciously uses his or her natural *instinct* to achieve a more successful way of life that benefits not only self, but mankind as a whole. Psychic ability is nothing more than instinct.

Take a momentary glance back into the dark ages of the first primitive existence of man. Animals were given instinct in order to survive, and so was man! Many animals instinctively know when to migrate with the change of seasons. Others can instinctively find food and water, or know when danger is near. This instinct was given the animal so it might survive in what, at the best of times, is a dangerous world.

At this same moment in time, the intellect of prehistoric man was not sufficiently developed to the degree that he could reason in a logical manner. The same nature that gave the animal the instinct needed to survive also gave that ability to man. This instinct enabled his species to survive.

As man continued to evolve and his thinking capacity increased, he developed other means of self-preservation and protection from danger: first the club, then the ax, the bow and then the rifle. As early man's means of protection became more sophisticated, he relied less and less upon his psychic abilities, or instinct.

A climax in the evolutionary cycle occurred when man experienced the first conflict between his rational, thinking mind and the mind that had been controlled by instinct. He had come to rely more and more upon what he could see, touch, taste, hear, and feel instead of what he previously had *sensed*. And it is quite understandable that our early ancestors would orient themselves toward this physical world instead of toward a world that was unseen.

Though our ancient forebears relied less and less upon their instinct, it was by no means lost. Instinct remains an integral part of our character and personality from the moment of our birth—when we *instinctively* begin our fight for survival. You may not be consciously aware of your instinctive ability, but I am absolutely convinced that this book will open wide the door to its positive recognition and to the logical use for which it was intended.

One argument raised against the use of psychic abilities is that we no longer need to use these abilities to warn of physical danger, to lead us to food or water. I disagree. We are always in constant danger of physical harm, and accidents and other acts of physical violence can be prevented by the proper use of the psychic ability that is readily at hand. But possibly more important than physical danger is the emotional and spiritual danger that is a part of so many lives today. We should be grateful that Nature was beneficent enough to keep instinct such a distinctive portion of our being. I would compare the person who does not utilize his psychic potential to a blind man who attempts to navigate an obstacle course, never sure where the next obstacle may be. Why should *you* walk as one blind when you have the ability to see your future and avoid obstacles without needless tripping and falling? Of course, psychic development in itself cannot remove the obstacles, but it can give you a warning of what lies ahead *before* you trip over it. It is this warning of what is before you that allows you to either adjust your stride or to change your course so that you avoid the obstacle entirely.

The advent of modern science did much to relieve man of the need to use his psychic abilities. We have thus been taught to disbelieve anything that cannot be written in a mathematical formula or proved by way of the five physical senses.

Fortunately, there have been scores of persons throughout the ages who have clung to the conviction that there is more unseen in the universe than can be seen. Jesus, Swedenborg, Andrew Jackson Davis, Stainton Moses, Sir Oliver Lodge, Sir Arthur Conan Doyle, and others have left us a wealth of evidence that supports a belief that man's instinct or psychic ability has never actually left him. By the way, if you are interested in ESP in a religious sense, and biblical examples of it, see the Appendix to this book, which discusses a number of biblical references.

Are Some People More Psychic Than Others?

From the experience I have gained during the past three decades, my answer would be yes! There are some individuals who do seem to have more natural abilities than others. There are those persons who come from families in which all the family members seem to be psychic. I am not convinced that this is entirely due to hereditary factors, however. It appears to be more a matter of environment. My best students have been from homes that have not necessarily believed in psychic phenomena, but neither have they scoffed at it. This tolerant attitude of the parent toward the entire psychic field during the child's youth appears to be a tremendous asset to the psychic learner—fostering the healthy attitude that all things are not probable, but they are possible. These students are not burdened by a closed mind.

Within my own family it was never thought of as eccentric or crazy to have knowledge of a future event. I can't say that the family always believed or followed their feelings, but there was no stigma attached to a person following a hunch.

The Scottish Presbyterian branch of the family called it "second sight." The Irish Roman Catholic branch referred to it as "the gift." My German Quaker ancestors called it "the curse"—not because it was evil, but because the psychic person would never have a life of his or her own. My English Episcopalian family used the words *the spirit*.

What's obvious from the preceding paragraph is that regardless of religion, they all believed in the psychic world. The only difference is that each branch of the family used a different term to describe the same thing.

The psychic students who seem to have the most difficulty utilizing their psychic faculties are those from homes where creativeness and imagination were frowned upon. In my own experience they not only have the most difficulty in using their psychic abilities, but also the most difficulty in adjusting to life itself. I recently counseled a lady, raised in this type of environment, who was going through a very torturous emotional period. She told me that she had had "second sight" throughout her life, but that because of the scorn of friends and family she did everything in her power to suppress it. I wonder whether if this lady had used, rather than subdued, her instinct she would not have found herself in such an emotional predicament. She confessed that she had known where her life was taking her, but would not pay attention to her intuition.

I felt quite sure that when she left me after the meeting, the warning signals of Nature would no longer go unnoticed or ignored.

Does Age or Sex Have Anything to Do with Psychic Development?

Neither age nor sex is a determining factor in psychic development. Rather, it all hinges upon open-mindedness and sincerity. I see many children and young people who do exceptionally well in using their psychic ability. Not as often do I see elderly persons making the same progress—due generally to the fact that the elderly person often loses interest in learning new things. The younger person is free of the many prejudices that sometimes plague the older person. Youth more readily adapts to learning and using things that are new and, to the individual, untried. Your own development is fundamentally determined by your mental age, not your chronological age. Recently I had a lady in one of my classes who was in her seventies and she did exceptionally well—a star pupil. She said, "It's never too late to learn, but I wish that I had done this years ago." She was mentally youthful and willing to learn—and she did!

Whatever your own age, this book can open new horizons of success and understanding. Keep an open mind and a willing heart and in but a short time you will be amazed at yourself as you grow to a wider and fuller dimension of right and happy living.

There are many readers who have in all probability known exceptional psychics, or have had friends or family whom they considered to be very gifted persons. Possibly you may feel that you could never be as psychically attuned as these others have been. You might rationalize that you would be wasting your time in developing your own psychic credentials unless you could be guaranteed that you would be the best in the world.

If this were a commonly held rationalization the entire world would be the less for it. The world needs those who are willing to rise to the challenge of progress. There would be no progress if you, or others, refused to develop your own talents. This reasoning is not only true for psychic development, but for the arts and the sciences as well. Much comfort, beauty, and knowledge have come into the world from others than the very "best" in their field—and honestly, you're the first and most important person who needs the help that psychic power can furnish. You can, and will, become an expert in meeting your own needs and having your own wishes fulfilled.

No two people have identical psychic ability, so don't expect to find it that way. One person will do better in psychometry, another in billet reading, and another in aura analysis; but all people can use the various psychic talents to the degree necessary to achieve their own personal desires.

Why not concentrate on one phase of psychic development? You may do the best in one psychic field, but you must know and learn to use all phases of your psychic ability before you can excel in the one psychic field you may consider your "psychic specialty." As you use all five of your physical senses to comprehend the physical world, so must you use all of your psychic senses to comprehend your psychic world.

Everyone Has Experienced a Psychic Impression

Each of you have received psychic impressions since birth. Unfortunately, many parents discourage their children from having an imagination. This is the beginning of the building of a wall that prevents the conscious acceptance of a psychic impression.

As a child, you may have hidden and subdued your instincts in fear of becoming a target of wrath or ridicule from other children as well as adults. Even today, in what is termed an "enlightened society," you will find parents who guide their children in the use of the practical side of the brain and ignore the creative/psychic portion of the brain.

Think back to your own childhood. Did you have imaginary playmates? Did you *sense* that certain adults, such as teachers, did not like you? Did you have a favorite pet that you just *knew* had something wrong with it when all outward signs showed it to be fine? I'm sure you can remember similar "childhood psychic experiences," because everyone has them.

Do you recall, as you grew older, just how difficult it became to relate your psychic experiences to those around you? As you became physically mature you probably laughed often at the active imagination you possessed as a child. But you really never outgrew those psychic impressions—you trained yourself not to consciously acknowledge or heed them.

Now you must "unlearn" that which caused a past reluctance to accept and understand those unseen forces that are such a natural part of each man and woman. You've delayed in using all of your unseen abilities, but they have not vanished from existence—they are only resting.

For various reasons many adults do not wish to use such terms as *psychic* or *ESP*. They prefer to use more commonly used and acceptable words. Ladies seem to prefer *women's intuition,* where the male of the species declares that he has a *hunch.* Regardless of the word you choose to use, psychic phenomena is a real and vibrant fact of life.

It would not be difficult to recall instances in which you were about to pick up the telephone to call a friend, and he or she called you first. How many of you gentlemen have had a "hunch" to call your wife before you left work, to hear her say, "I was hoping you'd call. Will you stop and pick up the cleaning?" or whatever? Ever know a fisherman who could catch his limit when no one else could get a bite? Ask him how he does it, and he'll tell you he had a "hunch" as to where the fish are and what bait they would best respond to.

Once my wife and I were on our way to a social gathering. Halfway there she said, "I shouldn't have worn this dress. Helen has a yellow one almost like it and she's going to wear hers." When we reached the gathering, sure enough, there stood Helen in her beautiful yellow dress. Helen's first comment to my wife was, "I told Frank you were going to wear your yellow dress and that I should change mine."

The above example might sound relatively unimportant, but if any such situation causes you a feeling of disharmony, it is very important and should not be brushed off as insignificant. If you are realistic about life I think you'll agree that it is the "little things" that can keep a person unhappy, and not constant catastrophes. Why not avoid these unpleasant annoyances when you already possess the ability to dodge them with some effective, psychic fancy footwork?

Thousands of psychic impressions have been received by my own family—many of them trivial (such as the dress affair), but others with a deeper and more important meaning. The first concerns the occasion of my brother's death.

In the summer of 1944 my brother was fighting with the 1st Army Division near St. Lo, France. My mother, early one July morning, said, "I know Walter is dead!" Though grief stricken, she hoped against hope that it was her imagination. Her instinct was correct, however, for three weeks later, her premonition was confirmed. You might ask how this knowing in advance helped her. The temperament of my mother is such that if she had not had the opportunity of this three-week adjustment before the confirmation of death, it could have meant total physical and mental collapse. Her forewarning added immeasurably to her ability to cope with the tragic passing of one so deeply loved.

I well remember my brother's last army leave before being sent overseas. As he walked away from our home for the last time, my grandmother said, "We'll never see him again." I remember well her answer when I asked her how she knew. "I just know it," she replied.

Another incident involved a cousin of my mother's who had a young son. From the time of his birth she maintained he would be a great musician. The mother began piano lessons for the boy at a very young age. She had a premonition that she would die while her son was still a child. She asked her husband, in-laws, and parents to promise that if anything happened to her, the boy's music lessons would continue. She died before his sixth birthday.

This young man has now written a score of operas and symphonies. He is the head of the music department at a large university. He has been guest conductor of a number of the largest symphony orchestras in America, and his career has just begun. Without his mother's psychic warnings, would a great musical talent have been lost to the world? I believe so. No other member of the family showed such musical talent, and I doubt that any of them would have thought to provide music lessons for the boy.

If there could be no practical benefits from the development of your psychic abilities, I would be the first to say "forget it." But the practical benefits of your psychic self-realization can be boundless. I will relate but a few of the everyday practical benefits that I personally received through my own psychic abilities.

I was driving on a San Francisco street early one evening on my way to attend a class at San Francisco State University. I was very relaxed and enjoying the beautiful spring evening. Suddenly, I heard a voice literally yell, "Stop!" I slammed on the brakes. In a matter of seconds two cars came racing through the intersection a few feet in front of where my own automobile had come to an abrupt halt. If I had ignored the voice, or if I had not been attuned to my intuitional world, I would have been hit broadside. I'm no expert on automobile accidents, but judging from the speed of the racing autos, the outcome of such a collision could not be happy. Instinct prevented an unnecessary tragedy.

Another time, the same month as the racing car incident, much to my embarrassment, I forgot the most basic of all good safety habits; I was not paying attention to what I was doing.

I was walking along the street daydreaming, fully enraptured by that spring feeling of just what a wonderful world I was living in (at that moment I didn't know how close I was to making *living* past tense). I had just begun to step from the curb to cross the street when a voice called my name. I stepped back onto the curb to greet whomever had called my name. As I turned, a city bus raced by and missed hitting me by inches. My life was saved again.

An interesting thing about this particular example was the fact that other people also heard the voice.

When I had turned to see who had called my name, I saw many people staring at the fool who almost became a part of the pavement. I didn't see a familiar face in the crowd, but I did want to thank whomever had called my name. When I asked, "Who called my name? I'd like to thank you," the people standing closest to me replied that they didn't know. They weren't even sure of where the voice came from—whether it was behind them, next to them, or in front of them.

Perhaps the voice was one of the onlookers', but it seems unlikely. There was no reason for anyone not to admit their assistance. Secondly, I'm positive that I was not even vaguely familiar with any person in that crowd.

Let me tell another story. I, my wife, and children were driving to Los Angeles from San Jose. As many are prone to do on California highways, I was traveling well over the speed limit. Suddenly a **feeling** of fear swept over me. So intense was the feeling that I immediately began braking to a halt. As I pulled to the side of the road, my speed now about thirty m.p.h., the right rear tire blew out. If I hadn't heeded my feeling, who can say for sure what would have happened? It certainly couldn't have been anything positive.

More recently, my son was to drive to a football game approximately fifteen miles south of San Jose. I received an impression that there was danger surrounding the trip. I discussed the matter with him, and he reluctantly agreed not to drive to the game. The next day we read in the newspaper about one head-on collision and several minor accidents that occurred at the very time, and at the very place, my son would have been traveling. Coincidence?

What is this psychic thing? It's a natural ability. It isn't a "gift," as many claim it to be. That would imply that Nature bestowed a reward upon "special" individuals. It has been my experience that all people are equal. Would you give one of your children a Christmas gift and ignore the other? Of course you wouldn't. Nature wouldn't either.

Factors That Hinder Psychic Development

If you were to take a few moments and ask yourself the question, "Why is it that I haven't been able to develop my psychic talents before?" your most honest response would probably be, "I haven't really tried."

There are mountains and mountains of misinformation on the subject of psychic development, and you've probably met scores of people who have told you of their own "supernatural" experiences. If you've had a bad experience with either camp, forget about it—clear your mind. To learn *ESP for Everyone,* you simply have to have an open mind and the desire to learn something new and different.

Love of the Mysterious

Quite recently, a student from one of my psychic development classes ssaid to me, "I'm convinced being psychic is natural, but I enjoyed it more when it seemed 'mysterious.' I still can't get used to the idea that you're simply human."

Almost everyone likes a little touch of the mysterious in their lives. It is this love of the mysterious and the supernatural that I've found to be one of the greatest hindrances to psychic development. I emphasize: Even though you may like the mysterious, remember that psychic development is not a mystery, and don't let yourself think otherwise.

I believe that as you progress through the lessons in this book, you'll come to that same conclusion.

Character Does Not Determine Psychic Ability

One evening while still in high school, I was leaving a movie theater just as one of the best woman psychics I knew was walking by. "Staggering by" is probably a better description of her movements. I had always assumed that talented psychics must be very special, very spiritual, and advanced far beyond the point of having the faults and frailties of the ordinary person. This experience was traumatic! It rocked the foundation of my previously held convictions.

As time passed, I observed that other very good psychics were human, with the same faults and the same strengths as the rest of us.

I began comparing the lives of famous artists and famous musicians. I found some of these great men to be almost saintly and others to be degenerates. Was their talent determined by character? Of course not! Much of their artistic talent was born to them.

Superstition as an Obstacle

The superstitious beliefs that surround psychic matters, I believe, can be traced to three main sources: dogmatic religions, the desire for the mysterious, and psychics themselves.

This is the very moment that *you*, as a learner, should use to develop a very healthy attitude toward psychics who demonstrate before the public. Some of them are wonderful and religious people, but there are those who have morals and scruples that might not be as highly developed as your own. Remember, psychic abilities are *not* determined by character. If you strike up associations with those in the psychic field, bear this fact in mind. I have known many people who have had unhappy experiences with psychics, and their opinion of the entire field is colored by them. This view is as ridiculous as the opposite extreme—that all psychics are perfect. You will have no difficulties if you remember that *psychic abilities are not determined by character,* and that psychics are natural, normal people.

Psychic Abilities Are Not a "Gift"

I believe that tradition is greatly responsible for the various psychic abilities that are referred to as *gifts.* This view of the psychic talents of various individuals can be a great hindrance to your own personal psychic development. Let's examine the implications of the word *gifts.* First, we infer that it is something only a select group of people have been chosen to receive. Your common sense will tell you that this is not true. Being psychic is natural and given to everyone. It cannot be considered a gift any more than could eyesight, hearing, or other physical senses.

It is unfortunate that many individuals who do use their psychic abilities to aid their friends or family, or in demonstrating before the public, do refer to their psychic abilities as "gifts." I try not to compare, but I do find the attitude of many psychics comparable to those of professionals who believe that no one else can do their jobs. They do not want to train other individuals to replace themselves. If this type of person admits that someone else can do their work, their "security blanket" is taken from them. Psychics are also human, and it stands to reason that some of them would also hang onto their "security blankets" as tightly as anyone else.

I personally object when people refer to my own psychic ability as a gift. This implies that I'm *different.* I don't feel different, and I'm not weird. I feel normal, and that is the attitude I intend to continue. I hope that when you have finished the lessons in this book that you will *not* refer to your psychic work as a gift, either.

Without becoming too controversial, I would call your attention to the religious dogmatist whose particular creed teaches that all psychic phenomena is "the work of the devil." They swear that insanity or possession is the natural reward for those who practice these "evil" doings. In my view they have unfortunately not reached a level of understanding that would allow them to recognize that psychic abilities and their creed are not necessarily in conflict. The charge that psychic investigation leads to insanity is frankly preposterous. As a matter of fact, the only thorough examination of this charge was made in England, where the results proved the contrary to be true.

Members of the scientific community visited all English asylums. When they asked which religion the patient professed to follow, spiritualists had the smallest percentage of inmates, compared to their number in the general population.

This condemnation of things psychic by certain religions does inspire fear in some individuals. Where there is fear, there is superstition. These superstitious beliefs and fear can be a great hindrance to achieving psychic development. Let your common sense determine whether creed and the psychic should be separated in your mind.

As I have mentioned earlier, the desire for the mysterious leads some people to give superstitious and supernatural connotations to occurrences that are quite natural. I have had many amusing moments resulting from this particular facet of human behavior. One incident that remains vivid concerns what was once a nervous habit. At times I have given psychic impressions to over a hundred people at one meeting. I did this by using billets (bits of paper upon which questions have been written). I would usually tear the billet to shreds before my psychic impressions were concluded. I did this simply because I didn't know what to do with my hands during the psychic reading. I had been doing this for years, when one night a student said to me, "When are you going to tell us the secret about tearing the billets?" This tearing of the billets was solely to keep myself occupied, but it evidently was given great importance by those watching. Without even trying, I had given an aura of the mysterious to my billet reading when there was nothing supernatural or mysterious about it whatsoever.

Another example of the difficulty people have in accepting the psychic as natural and unmysterious was brought forth in a summer trip I made to Long Beach, California. I thought it might be fun to visit a crystal gazer—not because I wanted my fortune told, but just to visit and exchange pleasantries. The fortune-teller and I hit it off immediately and found we had much in common concerning our psychic experiences. I asked her if she actually saw pictures in her crystal ball. She quite honestly replied that she did not. She was using the crystal ball as a point of concentration only. The crystal ball, incense, and talismans were only to please the customers. "I tried just sitting across the table from people and reading their fortunes, but I was starving to death," she said. "I bought a crystal ball, hung a chain around my neck, and my business increased over-night—it's what people want."

I do not mean to imply that this woman was dishonest, because she was not. The readings and psychic impressions she gave were excellent—she just had to surround them with superstition and mysticism before the public could accept them. It is this type of thinking that could hold your own psychic powers in check if you let it. Don't!

This very fine lady and I were in complete agreement on one particular point. And that is—

Psychics Cannot Tell Fortunes

It is a literal truth that "Fortunes are made, they are never told." Like it or not, there is a law of cause and effect that is very active in this world. What does this mean? Simply, it means, "What you sow, so shall ye reap." A psychic can only tell you what you, or others close to you, have built into your own future. A psychic cannot make any future event occur—he or she can only tell you what your *own* actions have built into your future. This is one of the most beautiful services that you as a psychic person can perform. You can warn individuals that certain of their actions are leading to certain consequences and thereby prevent danger or unhappiness.

Telling fortunes carries the connotation of psychics being able to make things happen—but they positively *cannot*. It is the individual person who can and does.

I hesitate to belabor the point, but it is extremely important that you, as a psychic student, fully realize that you cannot be psychically aware of any future event that has not already been placed in the future, by the thoughts or actions of people or as the consequence of a natural or spiritual law. This should help you also to understand why information concerning future events given you by a psychic, or information you may give to others as a psychic, does not always come true.

Here is an elementary example. Say an individual asks you the question, "Will I sell my car?" Your ESP tells you, and you respond, "Yes, you will sell it next Thursday." Later that evening the individual decides that he does not want to sell his car after all. Was the psychic impression incorrect? No, it was not incorrect. If the individual had not changed his mind, the car would most probably have been sold on Thursday as was predicted. *You can only read from the future those things already created by thought, action, or spiritual or natural law.*

Don't Confuse Being Psychic with Being Mediumistic

A psychic is one who through his or her natural, inherent powers is sensitive to nonphysical forces. Fundamentally, the psychic's mind moves toward the source of the information he or she is seeking, and through the use of his or her *psychic senses* comprehends and interprets the information psychically received. Psychic development needs a very active mind and nervous system. Mediumistic development is of a very passive nature. Being mediumistic means that you receive information from the spirit of a person who previously lived on earth.

This book deals with *psychic* phenomena, and you will find it much to your advantage to keep in mind that you are learning to use your *own* inherent abilities. Mediumistic development is achieved by different means than those described in this text. Since I myself possess certain mediumistic talents, I know there is a quite real difference between mediumistic and psychic abilities.

At one point in my psychic journey, I was a monthly television guest, along with my co-worker, Dave E., on a talk show broadcast from the San Francisco Bay Area. Our appearances were for the purpose of giving readings, or psychic impressions, to individuals within the studio audience, over the telephone, or from letters mailed to the studio—and it was live!

Both Dave and I found that we did our best psychic work when we were under the gun, so to speak. We also discovered that when it was necessary to give as many readings as quickly as we could, we relied solely upon our "instinct," or psychic abilities. We did not use any mediumistic ability.

Under other circumstances, when we were asked to give mediumistic demonstrations, it was a completely different experience, as we previously discussed. This was especially true when my wife, Dave, and I were invited to give demonstrations at various spiritualist summer camps. Spiritualists want to hear from spirits. They don't want ESP. There is a difference between being psychic and being mediumistic. Don't get the two confused.

I've been on television and radio in many places throughout the United States, and regardless of what the topic originally was, it always ended with my giving readings. It just seems that everyone is drawn to that—much like reading the horoscope in the newspaper. You may not believe in astrology, but I'll bet you read your horoscope.

There is Scientific Evidence

Experiments continue in the laboratories of some of America's finest universities. It would be foolish to say that scientists have found "all" the answers, but it's equally foolish to say that scientists have proved nothing.

It would take a very narrow-minded person to ignore, or reject, the laboratory experiments of Dr. J. B. Rhine and his wife at Duke University. Years of research went into their work. Their conclusions? There are such things as psychic phenomena. Dr. Rhine coined the now famous acronym "ESP" (extra-sensory perception).

The greatest evidence of all, however, still remains that which you have received for yourself, been given by a psychic, or evidence you have given to another. The real proof will consist in the abilities you learn to use through the eight weeks of lessons contained in this book. This will give you more than enough evidence to substantiate your own psychic abilities.

How to Begin Your Psychic Development

I have just attempted to call upon your common sense to be the guiding factor in your understanding of things psychic so that you might begin your development lessons with an open and balanced mind. I hope that many of the barriers to your progress have been removed and replaced with a proper understanding of the exciting psychic route to success that you are about to embark upon. A firm and realistic understanding of psychic phenomena will be a great benefit to you during your learning period, but most importantly, you will find it exceedingly beneficial in the future conduct of your material, emotional, mental, and spiritual endeavors.

I must be repetitious concerning one point: *I cannot make you psychic*. I can, however, show you how to develop and how to use the psychic ability that you *already* possess. At the end of the lessons, you will be amazed at just what a good psychic you really are. That is not the end of it, however. To become better and better at your psychic work you must continue with your psychic practice after you have laid the book aside. If you are like most novice psychics, this will not be difficult, as your friends and family will place a sufficient demand upon your abilities to ensure that they are not neglected. This book, as it is written, is identical to the method I use in conducting my own psychic development classes and it has proved to be very successful. I ask you to be sincere in your efforts and not to neglect what you might consider to be unneedful exercises, or to skip over the various suggestions that I will make to you throughout these pages. Be very conscientious in following the directions. Please don't be a mediocre student—you will receive mediocre results. Be a sincere and dedicated student, and you will be pleasantly surprised at the results.

Where to Begin

It is possible for you to follow the lessons as an individual, but much more preferable is to convene a group of people (two to ten) weekly for eight weeks. These group sessions will afford you the opportunity to practice as well as to learn from each other as your development progresses.

You might find that in the place of a weekly bridge game you might spend your afternoon working together on your psychic lessons. Maybe your Saturday night pinochle game could be rechanneled into a "psychic club." It's serious business, but it can be a great deal of fun as well.

When you begin your "psychic club," it should be understood by all that a somber attitude can be very detrimental to the psychic development of all concerned. What is needed is a lighthearted, happy atmosphere with plenty of laughter and good-natured fun.

How often have you felt happy and carefree, only to find that a few negative words from one individual threw you into a terrible mood? Unfortunately this can happen. Your club members should be in agreement that anyone who is in a pouty or unhappy mood *will not attend the meeting*. One person's bad humor can ruin your whole class session. Along the same line, when your group meets, keep the conversation light. There shouldn't be any discussions on what a lousy day someone had. Try to keep everything positive.

What Type of People Should You Invite?

The answer to that question is strictly up to you. Of course, you want people with whom you're compatible, people with whom you have something in common. Invite people you feel are average people.

Be aware that some people who are overburdened with problems attempt to learn about psychic phenomena in order to gain an advantage over others. They will not be good students and their negative attitude will hold everyone back from psychic fulfillment. People who are filled with hatred do not achieve psychic development. People who believe in witchcraft, superstition, and the like will also keep the group unbalanced. Beyond these caveats, anyone who will approach the coming lessons with an open mind will be an asset to your group.

Over the past years I've known many people who have taken psychic development classes, which were conducted by some of America's best psychics and/or mediums, and still failed to progress past the most elementary stages of development. There is one characteristic I've found to be common among these "dropouts," and this is their pessimism toward life and people in general—an inability to see the bright and good side of anything or anyone. The cause of their inability to use their psychic talents will never be known to themselves. They enjoy being miserable; perhaps they are fearful that the use of their psychic senses will make them see that it's a pretty good world after all. This type of person, quite frankly, is a hopeless case as far as psychic development is concerned. I advise strongly that you steer clear of this individual in all of your psychic work.

Meditation

The most common image of meditation is of the yogi sitting in the lotus position, eyes closed, completely oblivious to the world around him—lost in the great Universal Mind. This is a very good method for someone who is seeking to displace his consciousness from this world, or for someone who wants to become a medium. But this method is completely undesirable from the standpoint of psychic development. Earlier, I noted that your psychic abilities function through your nervous system—it is your nervous system that gives your psychic impressions meaning. In psychic development you do *not* want a disassociation of your personality from reality.

Meditation, for the purpose of psychic development, should simply be a quieting of the mind—the casting out of the troublesome and irritating thoughts of the day. When you have laid aside these encumbrances you have reached the state of mental harmony most conducive to rapid psychic growth. As you begin your lessons, you will be asked to take fifteen minutes each day to sit down, relax, and meditate the "psychic way."

How You Receive Your Psychic Impressions

We are aware that there is more unseen than seen within this universe. It is these "unseen" forces that carry the psychic impression to your conscious mind. An elementary example of these unseen forces at work is this: If you strike a key on the piano, it causes a vibration in the air. This vibration causes certain nerve reactions in your ear and brain, causing you to feel the note as a *physical sound*. The same procedure applies to a thought. The thought does not cause a vibration that can be comprehended by our physical senses, but it does cause a vibration that goes out into the universe to be understood by your five *psychic senses*. There is an unseen duplicate of each of your five physical senses that accepts and relays into your mind these unseen vibrations in much the same manner that the striking of the piano key relays the vibration to your physical ear.

When an unseen vibration comes into contact with your psychic senses, it causes an immediate reaction in your nervous system. The impression travels through your nervous system until it reaches your brain. The portion of your mind that accepts this information is the subconscious. How do you get the information from your subconscious mind into your conscious mind so that you might express it? You must revert to the old and much used method of "suggestion." You must constantly tell yourself that you can, at will, draw information from your subconscious mind into your conscious mind. Don't be haphazard about this—make it a ritual: *"I can, at will, draw any information I desire from my subconscious mind."* Say it again and again. You'll find that it works.

The drawing of this information from your subconscious mind is the area in which mistakes are made or wrong information sometimes given by professional psychics. You might wonder how some psychics can give amazing and verifiable predictions at one moment and in the next give completely erroneous information. The explanation is simple. They are misinterpreting the information they are drawing from their subconscious mind. I am completely convinced that no psychic impression is received incorrectly by the subconscious mind—the error lies in its conscious interpretation.

I know from experience how true this can be. I

have given literally thousands of psychic impressions in person, before groups, by mail, or via television or radio. My degree of accuracy has been proved, but I still find many times when I am completely wrong. My particular frame of mind, physical condition, and so on, all seem to play a part in accuracy. I quite frankly tell my classes and audience that I am not 100 percent correct—that no psychic is. If you receive a psychic prediction that makes sense, accept it until it proves itself to be correct or incorrect. It is only through practice and constant use that your own psychic accuracy will increase—the very same principle as in learning to use any ability. You must practice a great deal to become proficient.

Do Psychic Impressions Come to You?

Not necessarily! When you think of a particular person or situation at a distance, it is as if your mind travels to that location to receive the information. In fact, the vibrations you wish to contact surround the person or situation concerned. You must therefore travel to that person or situation in order to receive the proper impression. This is done without conscious effort on your part. The very act of thinking leads you to the proper source of psychic information.

The Role of Imagination

When you first begin to use your fullest psychic potential, don't expect flashes of light, skyrockets, or bells ringing, because they won't. Psychic impressions are very subtle experiences, and without practice you will find it very difficult to convince yourself that it isn't just all imagination. At this point don't refuse to accept what you are receiving by thinking your imagination is running wild.

The greatest obstacle I've noted in the psychic development of my own students is their fear of being ridiculed because of an overactive imagination. I so often hear a student say, "I don't want to say what I'm thinking because I'm afraid I'm imagining it." I always tell these learners that they are among friends, and who cares if they are right or wrong at this period in their class work? The important thing is to learn to express what you are, or think you are, receiving. The line between imagination and a psychic impression is so thin that only through practice will you recognize the difference. You will learn to distinguish between the two, so don't worry about it.

Psychic Terminology

You should familiarize yourself with these words and their meanings. I will be using this terminology throughout the following lessons.

Psychic (adj.) sensitive to nonphysical forces; (n.) one who through his or her soul, self, or mind can produce what are termed extrasensory phenomena.

Clairaudience ("clear hearing") the hearing of sounds from sources not physically present.

Clairvoyance ("clear seeing") seeing, or having "visions" of, objects not physically present.

Clairsentient having the power to discern objects and events not present to the physical senses.

Aura an electromagnetic force surrounding all physical objects.

Vibration a periodic impulsation or wavelike oscillation of electrical energy.

Symbol Something that stands for or suggests something else by reason of relationship or association.

Billet   a brief letter.

Psychometry   the divination of facts through the "soul" or the past of an object.

or

Reading or Message   a communication of psychic impressions and predictions.

Precognition   Knowledge of something before it occurs.

If you have the terminology firmly in mind, turn the page to begin your first psychic lesson.

Eight Weeks to Develop Your ESP

1

LESSON 1

The Importance of Vibrations in Psychic Development

Understanding vibrations is the first step toward the expansion of your new consciousness, your new intuitive abilities. It's near impossible to fine tune your instinct until you understand the importance of vibrations in all psychic development. If there were no vibrations, there couldn't be either a psychic or a physical world.

To function well in this world we need to know many things. Take mathematics, for instance. If you don't learn to add numbers, you can't subtract or multiply. Without addition, subtraction, and multiplication you could never learn to divide. Lack of this knowledge would certainly hamper the kind of growth and success most of us desire. Just as mathematics are needed for material success, a basic knowledge of vibrations is needed for psychic success.

You must first learn about vibrations before you can understand symbols, and symbols before you understand clairvoyance, clairaudience, and clairsentience. Each of the lessons that follow is a logically planned step that gives you complete, not partial, use of the instinctive powers that can make each day brighter, more prosperous, and happier. Partial development of your psychic abilities may be not only frustrating, but also a hindrance. Partial or incomplete psychic information can lead you down the wrong path, to unhappy consequences. You should desire to gain complete psychic knowledge, for it is there that you find the secret to spiritual and material enrichment.

Recently I watched a mother plead with her husband not to let their son drive the car. She didn't know why she felt this way and couldn't give the boy's father a reason for not allowing him to take the car. Fifteen minutes later a telephone call informed the parents that the boy had been in a serious automobile accident just blocks from home.

What was it this mother *felt* but couldn't put into words? Why didn't she sense *what* was going to happen, rather than just the feeling of danger? Could this accident have been prevented?

Of course the accident could have been prevented, and it should have been. A psychic warning was given and then ignored. The result of this unfortunate situation was injury and destruction—all because a vibration was ignored.

What Are Vibrations?

My definition of vibrations given in the previous chapter, "a periodic impulsation or wavelike oscillation of electrical energy," may not be as clear in your mind as I would like. You may have wondered what this has to do with psychic development. The definition also sounds relatively scientific to many a beginning student, but it is a literal truth that vibrations are everything. In this chapter I hope to acquaint you with the importance of vibrations in your personal and practical psychic development.

How Science Regards Vibrations

Science does have a law that explains, for its purpose, what vibrations are. It says that all matter is composed of atoms, neutrons, electrons, and protons. The manifestation or character of all matter is determined by how the neutrons and protons revolve within the atom. Science may at times use the word *energy* rather than *vibration*, but its meaning is the same. I would conclude with the scientist that there is but one force in the universe, but it is a force that expresses itself in various forms of matter.

How the Psychic Regards Vibrations

The psychic does not disagree with the scientific definition of vibrations, but I will elaborate on my first definition: *The first law of all creation is the energy called spirit*. This energy, or spirit, is manifested in an unseen way as well as through physical matter. Thus, a thought creates a vibration in the same way as the hammer that strikes the anvil. Vibrations are called by many names. Some call them energy, some spirit, and some call these vibrations God. Regardless of the word you choose to describe *everything*, there is nothing else.

It may be difficult for us to comprehend that every bit of matter—stone, wood, glass, metal, plants, or flesh—is formed by vibrating energy—atoms, neutrons, and protons. But because these things are composed of energy, they do vibrate. Every object's vibrations manifests its character by the type of energy it produces. Physically we cannot feel a sound in the air, hear a thought, or feel the magnetism of a magnet with our fingertips, but these vibrations do exist.

Vibrations travel through space in much the same manner that a ripple travels across water after you've dropped a stone into it. Vibrations travel in all directions, sometimes very rapidly and sometimes very slowly. The only difference between one kind of matter and another is simply the number and frequency of the vibrations that pass into or out of it.

Consider this fact: *Our bodies are composed of vibrations and we live in the midst of other vibrations.* Our minds, our bodies, and our spirits—in fact, the whole of existence—are merely one thing, vibrations.

Psychic vibrations are the same as such physical vibrations as radio and television transmissions. Psychic vibrations simply travel at a greater speed than physical vibrations.

An example of how physical vibrations come to us is seen if you go to your window and watch the automobiles driving up and down the street. The cars you see are of different colors, because what you perceive is the reflection of light at several different wavelengths. Now, that isn't mysterious, is it?

Nature blessed us with this gift of sight and the ability to visualize physical objects. It can be described in very complex terms, or as simply as I have just done. It depends on your point of view, but for the purpose of these lessons, it's best to keep it as simple as possible.

The vibrations of physical objects create mental images. Vibrations that are less concrete such as a thought, the future consequences of a present act, or vibrations of a physical act taking place at a distance that cannot be known by the use of physical senses, are received and comprehended through the use of your psychic senses, in much the same manner as you received the colored images of the automobiles with your physical sight. Receiving information psychically is no more mysterious than receiving information via physical senses.

When you consider that everything is composed of vibrations, the ability to attune to the unseen as well as the seen isn't as unreasonable as it may have seemed when you first began to read this chapter.

Vibrations through Psychic Senses

You have already learned that you receive psychic impressions (vibrations) by means of your psychic senses. Psychic senses are unseen duplicates of physical senses. Seeing the colors of the automobiles was a matter of vibrations acting upon your *physical* senses and making an image in your *conscious* mind. Psychic impressions are vibrations that bounce back from any place or thing you *think* about. Your reaction to vibrations from the unseen is the same as your reaction to the vibrations of the seen, except that the image of the former is first produced in the *subconscious* mind. The automobiles produced an image that appeared external, or at a distance from you. The psychic image can be seen either *objectively* or *subjectively*. In the case of a subjective image, it appears to be in the center of your forehead (often called the "third eye"). This internal or external image is apprehended through *clairvoyance*, which will be discussed in chapter two.

All of your psychic impressions are received because of your attunement with vibrations. Directing your thoughts to a person, place, or thing, your mind, which is not restricted by distance, "reaches out" to mingle with the vibrations from what you are thinking of. Thus, your psychic impression is carried to your subconscious mind where it either produces an image (clairvoyance), a sound or sounds (clairaudience), or a feeling (clairsentience).

I have so far discussed vibrations mainly from a physical point of view. There is, however, another popular point of view, the religious one. Your own common sense should dictate which theory you choose to accept or reject. I see no conflict between the various views of the origin of vibrations.

A Religious Point of View

To explain the religious view of vibrations, it is necessary to go back briefly to the creation of the world. The Book of Genesis from the Bible states that "In the beginning there was God." We go on to read that God then created the world and all living things during seven days. The religionist asks the question, "If in the beginning there was God and nothing else, what did He create the world out of?" An assumption is that He must have created all things from Himself. Hence, all things in the universe are God, each a different expression of Him.

You are probably familiar with the widespread teaching that there is nothing in the universe but God. This belief is prevalent in most Oriental religions as well as in the newer Western churches. Those who accept the theory that vibrations are different manifestations of God generally believe that psychic phenomena are a result of the God within you recognizing the God in another person, place, or object.

I leave it to you to choose between religious theories, a combination, or none of them. Regardless of your own particular standpoint on the matter, however, keep in mind that vibrations absolutely exist. Your opinion, whatever it is, cannot erase the fact of their existence, nor can it change their character. *Vibrations are everything.*

How to Be at the Right Place at the Right Time

Many an executive has attributed his success to being at the right place at the right time. Granted, they must have recognizable ability before they are promoted, but what of those who have similar ability but are overlooked for promotions?

Steve was working in the production control department of a large manufacturing company. He liked his job, but he had a growing feeling that he should make every effort to move into the manufacturing area of the company—an area in which he had had no previous work experience. Steve followed his hunch. He talked with his supervisors about making the career change.

Steve had no apparent reason for requesting the new job assignment, which would necessitate a demotion. He could only say, "I just believe that it would be in the best interests of the company and of myself to make the change." Steve was at last given the transfer. Within one year, Steve himself was promoted to the management team.

Steve explained his success in this manner: "I followed a hunch, and that hunch put me in the right place at the right time—it was a matter of timing. It was the smartest move I ever made, but I needed constant reassurance from my wife that sometimes it's necessary to take one step backward in order to take two steps forward."

Let me give another example. A small church was

holding services in leased quarters. A sudden urge to move to new quarters swept the church—but it was impossible. Their lease ran several months before it expired, and there was no hope that the landlord would cancel the lease.

In the meantime, unknown to the church congregation, their landlord had been contacted by a real estate firm that wanted the building for a new franchise office—and they were offering a much higher rental than was being paid by the church.

The landlord asked the congregation if they would find new church quarters if he paid all moving fees and so on. The congregation agreed to move within thirty days, even though they had not even looked for a new church location.

Within a week the congregation found an empty building that contained not only a kitchen and nursery school, but offices on the side street that could be rented out.

Because of a complicated legal action, the building had long stood vacant. It was rented to the church on a month-to-month basis for a small, token payment. Several months passed before the divorce proceedings were concluded.

At the conclusion of the legal action, the $125,000 building was offered for sale to the church—with no down payment and monthly payments that were less than their previous rent. The unexplainable urge felt by the congregation was the prelude to what they could only term a miracle.

When you have feelings similar to Steve's and the church congregation's, pay attention! You are attuned to vibrations that are leading you to a richer and more abundant life. Being at the right place at the right time doesn't happen by chance.

How to Avert Approaching Danger

It is a very rare occasion when you do not receive a forewarning of approaching danger. The potential problem lies in your refusal to pay attention to the warning. In our previous example, because the mother couldn't give a rational explanation as to why the boy shouldn't drive the car, the father allowed it. But the serious accident could have been averted.

Bess knew she shouldn't drive to Los Angeles—she just had a *feeling*. She wanted to go so badly that she ignored the vibrations that were bombarding her and made the trip anyway. She spent six hours in a ditch before she was finally rescued from her accident.

Dave, on the other hand, was driving to Las Vegas. As he was about to go over a rise in the road, the *feeling* came over him that he should slow down. As he proceeded slowly over the rise he saw a car and trailer blocking the road. If he hadn't had the urge to slow down, or if he hadn't acknowledged it, what would have been the outcome? Dave paid attention to vibrations, and the vibrations served him in return.

How to Feel Harmonious with Your Surroundings

How often have you, for no apparent reason, felt nervous and upset? How often have you felt uncomfortable in a friend's home? How many times have you had a negative feeling about people, even before you met them?

Everyone has experiences such as these occasionally, but if they happen on a frequent basis you can be sure that you do not have a sense of harmony with people, things, or places.

There is usually no reason for you to dislike people, or for them to dislike you, upon a first meeting. The conflicted or negative feeling that you may have before meeting someone is caused by a difference in the vibrations between yourself and the other party. Before the meeting takes place, you should take a moment. During this quiet time you should concentrate on having your vibration harmonize with the vibration of the person you are about to meet. It takes two to make an argument or a conflict, so you can make sure your half will not participate. Then proceed to your meeting with your happiest smile—knowing that you're on your way to greet a new friend.

A few hours spent as a guest in a home where you feel great mental discomfort can seem an eternity. Not only that, but it can leave you with a feeling of complete exhaustion. You need not experience this discomfort again. Before you enter any new dwelling, you should again take a few quiet moments to project your vibrations into the home, so that when you enter you are immediately met with a feeling of friendliness, comfort, and rapport. When in the home, place your hand upon various objects and mentally say, "I feel love vibrating from this object, and I respond with love."

You must be the master of overcoming negative vibrations wherever you meet them. One simple, affirmative thought will harmonize the vibrations of any person, place, or thing—"I project love and I shall feel love in return."

Most mental and emotional anguish is the result of an inability to cope with things you feel but cannot understand. It is sometimes very sad to see people so emotionally mixed up and unhappy, when the tool to conquer this negativity is so close at hand. I believe it's overlooked because of its simplicity—it's not complicated enough to draw the attention. Surely there must be a mystery! Nothing so simple as projecting harmonizing vibrations could work! Give simplicity a chance. It *does* work. Give credence to an old adage: Truth is simply wonderful, and yet so wonderfully simple.

An Individual Exercise to Increase Your Psychic Sensitivity

Take fifteen minutes daily to quiet your mind. During this time touch various household objects. Lay your hand upon wood, metal, and glass. If you prefer the outdoors, touch a flower, a tree, the earth, or a simple garden weed. You will have a physical sensation—of heat, moisture, graininess, or whatever. And if you concentrate—and this is the key to the exercise—you will find these objects give you an inner *feeling*—the sensation of differences in the vibration of the various objects you touch.

You may become bored with this exercise and think that doing it once is sufficient. It isn't! Please do it daily for one full week. There are several reasons for this exercise, and you should avail yourself ot its benefits. First, developing this *feeling* for the things around you is the first step toward developing clairsentience. Second, it harmonizes you with your surroundings. Your conscious effort to feel the character of the things around you leads you to loving those things. Believe it or not, when you love your surroundings, your surroundings love you in return.

It would be a good idea to begin keeping a notebook of your experiences. Carefully note all of your thoughts and feelings. This notebook should be continued through these eight weeks of lessons. Keep notes on your group sessions and on your psychic experiences outside during the rest of the week. It will later prove to be an invaluable reference tool.

A Group Exercise to Increase Your Sensitivity

When your group meets for their first "working" session, you may find it very difficult to keep the members on the track. Some people are very inclined to get over-anxious. This exuberance is commendable, but attempting to jump ahead invariably leads to disappointment in this case. They must learn first lessons first.

Gather various objects from your home or garden so that you have one of each for every member present. Some objects you might use are flowers, glasses, matches, toothpicks, envelopes, stamps, feathers, salt, sugar, or pencils. There are hundreds of suitable objects within a home.

Your first step is to give each member of the group a match, for example. Have the group sit for a few moments with eyes closed. After all is quiet, each member should tell of the *feeling* they receive from that object. Do the same with each object.

Two hours is a sufficient length of time for your group to sit. If it is longer people will become tired as well as bored—though there are always those who become so enthralled with their new adventure that they'll keep you up all night talking (I speak from experience, believe me). This really is not a beneficial beginning to serious psychic study.

Each member of the group should also do the individual exercise described on p. 43 for the ensuing week. If anyone is unable to follow the course faithfully, politely suggest that he or she quit attending your sessions.

What you're doing may not make complete sense to you at present, but it will as the lessons progress—just take my word for it for now.

On the Road to Gain

Some very interesting things have happened to my students while carrying out this particular exercise, and you might find their experiences of value to you.

Anna could never grow a flower garden that suited her. No matter what she did, or how hard she worked, the neighbors' gardens were superior to hers.

As her exercise, she walked around her garden and tried to feel what was different in each flower variety. Each day as she stroked the blooms, she was aware of a feeling of real love for each individual plant. This feeling gave her such inner warmth that she continued long after the exercise week had ended. Suddenly, as if a miracle, new growth, color, and vitality were seen in her garden. "You know, Bob," she said, "it's true that you can feel vibrations from things. Love really does respond to love."

Another lady who was having marital difficulties decided that the objects of her exercise would be belongings of her husband. She brought her notebook to class at the end of the week for me to read. The first two days went something like this: "Monday: pipe—nervousness; comb—dislike; aftershave—jealousy. Tuesday: magazine—sinking feeling; beer bottle—dizziness." Her daily notes continued in this negative vein for the entire week.

It doesn't take a trained psychic to recognize the difference between the feelings of this particular lady, and say, those of the lady who loved her plants. Her notebook was filled with the feelings of a jealous, possessive wife toward her husband—she was not feeling the character of the items at all. She felt only her own inner negativity. This can be a real pitfall for the beginning student. This woman was unable to quiet her mind or harmonize her feelings before she began her daily exercises. And so psychic development was really out of the question for her—she was not strong enough mentally or emotionally to let go of her baser feelings.

Here is an example of how personal feelings can have a more positive effect on things around you.

My wife and I were at a garden nursery buying fruit trees to plant at the back of our house. In a gesture of kindness, the nurseryman offered my wife a small indoor plant that was going to be discarded because it was slightly misshapen. My wife liked the plant very much and took it home. It grew unbelievably, and it became a very attractive plant. My wife decided she'd like to share its beauty, so she moved it to the lobby of our church. The plant continued to grow until it reached a size that made it get in the way of members entering and leaving the church. Suddenly the plant began to die, and it was without sadness on the part of the many members who had had to dodge around it to enter the church. My wife moved the plant back home. Within days it was again thriving.

It seems obvious to me that the annoyance of church visitors had its effect on the plant, and as soon as it was removed, it thrived again. Thoughts and feelings—vibrations—are very real things, and they do register in the universe as surely as material objects.

The two preceding examples do concern vibrations, but somewhat in reverse. For the purposes of this lesson, however, it is necessary that you do *not* direct your feelings *to* an object, but rather allow feelings to come to you *from* the object. Differentiating between your own feelings and those that come to you from objects might be a bit difficult at the beginning, but persist in your practice.

Have you ever wondered why you like certain colors and not others? Why is it that everyone doesn't like the same colors? Each color is a reflection of a different vibration, and your favorite colors are those that are closest to your own individualized vibration.

It is this effect of color that will explain your group exercise turning up a great variety of feelings concerning a single object. Take for example a simple match with a red-and-blue striking head. If one person's vibration is entirely in attunement with red and blue, he or she might say, "I feel warmth, vitality," or the like. Another person who does not like those colors might feel coldness or weakness. Trained psychics will not be influenced by their personal likes and dislikes, but an untrained individual will naturally feel these differences. Don't be dismayed or wonder who is correct and who isn't during this first lesson—you're just beginning on a new and exciting adventure.

At the end of the first week, you should feel more secure and peaceful. You will avert danger because you will be paying attention to the vibrations protecting you. You may have more friends and should be forming a new and more prosperous future job plan. Don't wait for success to find you. Use the small amount of psychic knowledge I've just given you. Begin looking for success, happiness, love, and prosperity—and expect to find it!

DON'T GO ON TO THE NEXT
CHAPTER UNTIL YOU HAVE
FOLLOWED THIS LESSON
FOR ONE WEEK.

2

LESSON 2

How to Develop the Powers of Clairvoyance, Clairaudience, and Clairsentience

---

Before reaching the conclusion of this lesson, you'll have discovered one of the great secrets of genuine psychic development. It just isn't as startling or unusual as you might be led to believe. The use of your five physical senses is not a cause of wonder—and neither is the use of your psychic sense. The use of your psychic senses will come to be natural, because that's exactly what it is—a natural expression of yourself. There's nothing weird or supernatural about it at all.

The first psychic talent, or instinct, you'll learn about in this chapter is clairvoyance. To thoroughly understand clairvoyance you must first experience it, and that is exactly what you are going to do.

Clairvoyance

Figure 1 is a drawing of a simple flower. Take a look at it.

Now, close your eyes and visualize the same flower in your mind. If you have difficulty visualizing this flower with your eyes closed, open your eyes and study the picture again. Close your eyes again and visualize. This mental picture is exactly how a clairvoyant vision will appear to you as you progress through these lessons.

THE THIRD EYE

The mental picture of the flower most probably appeared to be located at the center of your forehead. This centered location of visualization is commonly referred to as the "third eye." It would be quite correct if you chose to use this same term, although I personally use it infrequently in teaching commonsense psychic development. It has become an overused phrase in forms of mysticism not relevant to the present subject.

SUBJECTIVE AND OBJECTIVE CLAIRVOYANCE

Again look at the drawing of the flower and visualize it in your mind. As the vision emerges within your mind above and behind the bridge of your nose, mentally move the picture so that it is visualized in front of you—outside the confines of the mind. You have now experienced both *subjective* and *objective* clairvoyance. Subjective clairvoyance is visualization within the mind, while objective clairvoyance is visualization outside of the mental confines of the head.

It is possible that you experience subjective clairvoyance with ease, but have difficulty experiencing objective clairvoyance. You may discover the opposite to be true. Or again, you may attune to objective and subjective clairvoyance with equal ease. It makes no difference! One form of clairvoyance is not superior to the other. It really does not matter where you see your vision. Later you may even see objective and subjective clairvoyant pictures simultaneously—creating a double-image effect. Don't get hung up attempting to discern *why* you experience clairvoyance in the manner you do. The question has no satisfactory answer, and this is not the proper time to lose your mind in philosophical meanderings.

Within most psychic circles, the words *clairvoyance* and *vision* are synonymous. One person may say, "I had a vision of . . ." while another may say, "I saw a clairvoyant picture of . . ." Both had the same psychic experience. They differ only in the way they express it.

Try the clairvoyant exercise described on p. 50 again. But instead of the flower, concentrate on the drawing of the simple tree in figure 2. Look at the tree. Practice both objective and subjective clairvoyance with your eyes tightly closed.

(The only reason you are directed to close your eyes is to simplify your concentration by blocking out the physical sensations that command your physical vision. Later you will discover that your visions are experienced as easily with your eyes open as when they are closed. No one will need to tell you when this point in your development has been reached. You will automatically open or close your eyes without conscious thought. You will, in an unconscious manner, meet the needs of the particular moment.)

When you feel comfortable with your visualization of figure 2, read on.

In many instances, clairvoyant visions will not look like the simple forms or objects you have practiced with. They may be entire scenes that are quite complicated. When this type of vision occurs to your consciousness, concentrate on the most striking details of the experience. Most visions are fleeting and you just will not have the time to concentrate on every detail of your clairvoyant picture. The "highlights" of the vision are what contain the vital psychic information that is seeking acceptance by your conscious mind.

Now concentrate upon the more complicated scene pictured in figure 3. Spend as much time on this visualization exercise as your own instinct dictates.

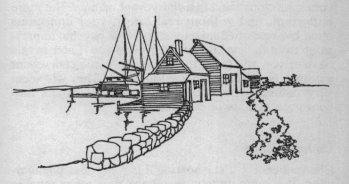

At this point the amount of time spent in your visualization is of little consequence, but developing a habit of spending a great deal of time in studying each vision will seriously hinder your later psychic development. True clairvoyant experiences are rarely the "seeing" of one picture. True visions are more commonly a rapid sequence of pictures that tells an entire story or points to a fully understandable revelation. A conscious effort to hold on to a single clairvoyant picture leaves no room for acceptance of the remaining pictures being "quick-fired" from your subconscious to your conscious mind. The result of hanging on to a vision? Inaccuracy of the psychic prophecy or revelation.

Many of my students have commented that their visions at first appear "fuzzy." They can see the vision, but not as clearly as expected or as is acceptable. If you experience this "fuzziness," don't worry about it. As you practice, these less than clear images will be replaced by clear, sharp visualizations.

By concentrating on these three drawings, you will become familiar with what to expect from, and how to accept, the psychic impressions that appear to your conscious mind in a clairvoyant manner. But more important, and without real effort, your conscious mind has relearned how to accept true psychic impressions from the psychic world around you. Later in this chapter you will learn to receive authentic clairvoyant pictures. No, they will not astound you. They will seem very natural experiences, not strange intruders into your present state of existence.

Clairaudience

Clairaudience ("clear hearing") is a peculiar phenomenon. It is more difficult to acquire than other psychic abilities, though I have discovered no real reason why this should be so. Among my students I have noted more psychological barriers to clairaudience than to any other psychic ability. It seems that the hearing of sounds from sources not physically present is more difficult to accept than other phenomena, although this need not be the case. It may have something to do with a childhood fear that is still unconsciously present.

In physical hearing, the reception of sound is caused by a vibration of the tiny hair cells within your ear. It is possible that sounds heard via clairaudience could be produced in the same manner—although evidence does not support this explanation. Psychic sounds are on a much higher vibrational level and do not have the force to create a physical vibration within the ear. It is for this reason that clairaudient sounds are generally heard subjectively rather than objectively, although in many instances the student is unable to discern which.

Another peculiarity of clairaudient development is the almost universal recognition that clairaudient sounds are heard within one ear only. Your first exercise in awakening your clairaudient abilities is to first discover which ear is your psychic ear.

A PRACTICAL METHOD TO DISCOVER YOUR PSYCHIC EAR

You will look rather strange when performing the following exercise, but I have found no easier or more practical manner by which to make this discovery.

Begin your exercise by sitting in a comfortable chair with a water glass placed firmly over each ear. Relax. As you sit quietly, listen intently for any type of sound. You may hear voices, running water, music, or any other sound that you are accustomed to hearing. (Don't expect to hear "unnatural" sounds. You won't! The hearing of unfamiliar sounds would have no psychic value. If you couldn't understand the sounds, they would be of no practical value in your development.)

As the sounds begin, pay very close attention to which ear is receiving the strongest noise. This reveals your psychic ear. Remove the glasses from your ears. To keep out unwanted sound while you continue your clairaudient exercise, place some cotton in the ear that heard less. By blocking this "weak" ear, you can more easily concentrate on what is being heard in your psychic ear.

The sounds, noises, or voices that you are now hearing psychically for the first time will have very little immediate meaning. They will have a great deal of meaning when you have reached the end of this chapter. In a few days you will be giving prophecies and predictions in the same manner, and with the same accuracy, as the "professionals."

Clairsentience

Lesson One was developed to increase your clairsentient ability—an ability that you have been using throughout your life.

Clairsentience is such a natural part of your being that it's probably become "old hat." Who hasn't had a certain feeling about a person, place, or thing? I've yet to meet the person who has not had these experiences, and I'd bet that you haven't either. These "feelings" are clairsentient experiences. As your lessons progress, you will use your clairsentient talent to recognize the past, and also the present, vibrations of things and people—what and who are beneficial to be around, and those that aren't. You'll use your clairsentient ability to *feel* your way through every day of your life.

The first lesson, on vibrations, instructed you to practice feeling positive vibrations surrounding various objects. There are, however, vibrations that are not always of a positive nature. In this week's lesson, conscientiously make yourself aware of negative feelings. But do not become so engrossed in the exercise that you make the negative a part of your own existence. Acknowledge the negativity, but do not accept it as your own. *You must supervise your own emotions.*

HOW TO BECOME ECCENTRIC

Without willpower and common sense, you can become overly sensitive to the plight of others. Sympathy is a prized emotion, but empathy is not always an admirable personality trait. Do not make the unhappiness of others your own unhappiness. No matter how worthy your intentions, you're playing the wrong ball game. You do not possess the right to usurp the happiness that belongs to another, and you likewise do not possess the right to absorb their unhappiness. If you continue down this rough and crooked road you will become eccentric at the least, schizophrenic at the worst.

MENTAL TANGLES YOU MAY ENCOUNTER

Generally speaking, your clairvoyant, clairsentient, and clairaudient lessons bring pleasure and peace; but you may experience sensations that *appear* to be negative, although they are not.

You may feel very negative the first week or two of this psychic program. You may find yourself moody, short-tempered, and irritable. This is, however, short-lived and its origin obvious.

First, you have just begun to use your previously dormant psychic abilities. This moodiness is akin to having sore muscles after strenuous exercise. True, you're uncomfortable, but the discomfort is quickly over.

Or look at the problem like this. What would happen if you were to awaken one morning to find that you had grown a third arm? It would certainly test your nerves until you learned to use it. You've acquired new talents, but you're still learning how to use them. It is not negative or unnatural for you to feel a certain amount of nervousness during this learning period.

If you are one of those individuals who feels irritable and negative, don't get hung up on wondering why. Use your willpower to overcome the brief inconvenience. Believe me, the unwelcome feelings last only a short time.

Learn to "Turn On" and "Turn Off" Your Psychic Impressions

There have been instances in which students have concentrated so deeply while performing the clairvoyant exercises that the pictures just seem to stick within them. They see the pictures at unexpected moments or wake during the night with the pictures in their consciousness. Why does this happen? Simple.

The healthy approach to psychic development is a sincere but casual attitude. Total immersion in the subject is not mentally healthy. You *can* try too hard! There is a time to turn it on and a time to turn it off. More appropriately, "turning it off" means allowing your conscious mind to subdue your subconscious mind. "Turning it on" is the simple act of allowing your subconscious mind to dominate the conscious mind. You cannot forget that you live in a physically oriented world. And you cannot hide from the responsibilities of that world by escaping into the subconscious. Use your psychic abilities in a sane and commonsense manner. Psychic ability should allow you to overcome problems, not escape them.

Individual Exercises

First Day

Practice building the image of the chair in your mind's eye.

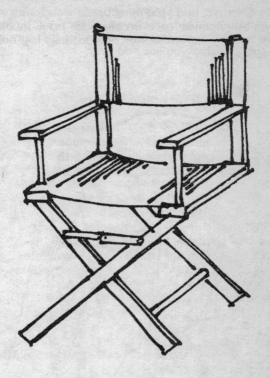

Now relax. Put the chair completely out of your mind. Close your eyes and relax. Say, "I want to see a picture." As soon as the vision has built itself within your mind, stop. Use your notebook to write down a description of your clairvoyant experience. At this time, don't ponder the interpretation of your vision—you'll learn how to interpret it in the next chapter. For now, let the vision go.

Sit quietly and *listen*. Do you hear anything in or about your psychic ear? Jot it down in your notebook.

Second Day

Treat this image, and those for the week's remaining days, in the same manner as on the first day, making notes on what you see and hear.

Third Day

Fourth Day

Fifth Day

Sixth Day

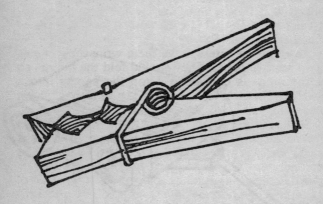

Group Exercises

Before beginning these weekly group exercises, make certain that each member has completed the preceding individual exercises before being admitted to the group meeting. If even one person hasn't done so, the group might as well simply have a party. The group exercise just can't be done unless each person has done his or her homework.

As everyone enters, have them write their names on two slips of paper. They should fold the papers so that the name is concealed. Drop the papers into a bowl. These "billets" will be used at a later time during the session.

Seat your group and ask them to relax. Place an object in the center of the group and practice "building images," just as you did in Lesson One. After ten to fifteen minutes of this exercise take a breather.

When the group is ready to begin the next phase of the exercise, the host or hostess should pass the bowl containing the previously written billets around the circle, asking each person to draw out the piece of paper. *Do not open the billet at this time.*

No one likes to be the first, so use some method to determine who is going to "read" the first billet (the excuses you'll hear for not being first become hysterical). Or, to save everyone embarrassment, why don't *you* just be first? Now begin the "readings."

Step 1: The first designated "reader" (Person A) holds the folded billet between his or her palms and silently says, "I want to see a picture." (Close your eyes if it helps your concentration.)

Step 2: When the clairvoyant picture has grown within his or her mind, Person A should describe the picture out loud. (No comments should be made by any member of the group until the description has been completed.)

Step 3: The reader should then mentally say, "I want to hear something." (Reader: Listen closely for a few moments. Remember, you may hear clairaudiently from without as in normal hearing, you may hear it down inside your ear, or you may not be sure where the sound is coming from—but the *where* doesn't make any difference.) After a description of what was heard, go to the next step.

Step 4: When Person A has finished describing what he or she heard and saw as he or she held the billet, Person A should now open the billet to discover who they were reading for—we'll now call that individual Person B (In your groups you'll use the names of the individuals.)

Step 5: Person A and Person B should now discuss Person A's clairaudient and clairvoyant impressions. It's the perfect time to check for accuracy—does the "message" make sense, and so on—but remember, this is a practice and a learning session. Don't expect perfection. You must also remember that even if the reading doesn't seem accurate, it may be. You may be reading about the past and about the future as well as the present. Only by practice will you learn to recognize the difference.

Step 6: Person B now draws a billet from the bowl and follows the preceding five steps to read for Person C. Continue this procedure until each person has given, and received, a reading. Remember to keep a record in your notebook of the billets and the psychic impressions they generated.

Suggestion: You may want to limit the amount of time for each reading and individual discussion to perhaps ten to fifteen minutes, or you're likely to watch the sunrise together.

The pictures and sounds you've received during this meeting are true clairvoyant and clairaudient experiences. Feels pretty natural, doesn't it?

DO NOT CONTINUE WITH
THE NEXT CHAPTER UNTIL
YOU HAVE DONE THE INDIVIDUAL
EXERCISES FOR ONE WEEK.

3

LESSON 3

The Importance of Symbols in Commonsense Psychic Development

The universal language of the psychic world is symbolism. The visions of the great prophets, seers, and mystics of both the past and present have been of a symbolic, allegorical nature, the visions of Nostradamus being classic examples.

The interpretation of symbols from the universal psychic language is the object of this lesson. And you will discover that it's not as mysterious or as difficult as it may sound on the surface.

I do not contend that every vision or clairvoyant experience will be allegorical in nature, but 99 percent of them will. At this point in your own psychic development, however, don't be concerned with the nuances that differentiate one from the other. You will soon be able to recognize the difference between a vision that is allegorical and one that is literal—and it is not that difficult.

What You Learned from Your Previous Lesson

During the group exercise your subconscious mind dominated your conscious mind to produce authentic symbolic visions that enabled you to give prophecies concerning the future and/or psychic readings, or impressions, of the present. You were instructed *not* to interpret your clairvoyant pictures at that time. The information in this lesson will now allow you to do so. Those pictures you saw, but did not intrepret, were *symbols*.

What Is a Symbol?

A symbol is *something that stands for or suggests something else by reason of relationship or association*.

Please note that the definition says, "stands for or suggests *something else*." This means that your clairvoyant visions mean something other than their literal appearance.

"A Picture Is Worth a Thousand Words"

It's an old saying, but it's true! Have you ever looked at a painting and seen an entire story on the canvas that goes beyond the one scene or object captured within the frame? It is the same with clairvoyant psychic impressions. You will most often see one symbol (or group of symbols) that convey a complete thought or story. What might, under other circumstances, take hundreds of words to describe can be given to you almost instantaneously via symbolic clairvoyant visions.

Many psychics, and some scientists, believe that man will evolve to a level where all communication will be mental rather than verbal. They believe that these telepathic thought forms (symbols) will be the method of communication between individuals. Telepathic communication does presently occur between people, but it is far from a universal phenomenon.

Back to your picture. What does it mean to *you?*

Symbols Mean Different Things to Different People

Each person's life experience is vastly different from anyone else's. These individualized past experiences allow each of us to develop our own symbolic languages. For instance, when I see a bell clairvoyantly I immediately know that it means victory. But a bell will not necessarily symbolize the same thing for you.

A friend of mine lived next door to a church for many years. Each Sunday morning the church bells began to ring promptly at nine A.M. For my friend, who liked to go dancing and drinking each Saturday night, the bell was hardly a symbolic sign of victory. It was an annoyance and an aggravation. And that is exactly what a bell symbolized when he was receiving psychic impressions. To you it might mean religion, school, punctuality, or any number of things. Its interpretation is entirely dependent upon your own past experience.

It is not possible for me to tell you what each individual symbol means to you; but for illustrative purposes I will describe three symbols that commonly apear to me.

A pine tree. This symbol means strength in a person. Therefore, if I see a pine tree standing erect, it means a person of sturdy character. If the pine tree is seen lying on the ground, it signifies that a person thought to be of strong character has proved to be a disappointment. If the symbol is moving away from me it means that a person previously relied upon is leaving. If moving toward me, it means that a person of such character is moving into my world.

A bee. The bee, to me, symbolizes prosperity. If the bee is visualized moving away from me, it denotes a loss. If the symbol moves toward me, it signifies that new prosperity is coming to me.

Hands. If the hands are not moving, there is a loss of work or no work at all at the present time. If moving, there will be no loss of work, or a new job is in the offing.

Using the three symbols above, I can give an example of a complete psychic reading. This is what I might see clairvoyantly.

A bee

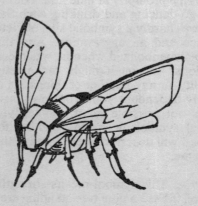

Busy hands

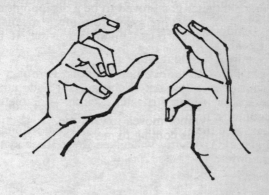

Pine trees

The psychic reading would be as follows: "I see prosperity coming to you [the bee flying toward me] through a work vibration [moving hands] where you have confidence or respect in two individuals [the two pine trees]."

See how simple it is?

Let's look at three other symbols: February 13—just what it says, the date February 13; a mountain—success after a long struggle; a circle—completeness or accomplishment.

Assume that you are giving a psychic reading and have just clairvoyantly visualized these three symbols in this order:

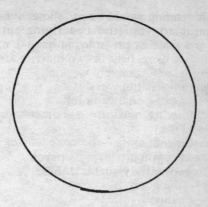

The psychic reading would be: "I see that on February 13 you will achieve or complete [the circle] that for which you have been struggling [the mountain]."

You may feel that reading symbols is too easy, or that the psychic impression is too short. But remember that it isn't necessary for worthwhile things to be difficult, nor is it necessary to take five minutes to answer a question that could be handled in thirty seconds. Finally, it is *not* necessary for you to know what you are reading about. The important thing is that the person for whom you are giving the reading understand it. I have no interest in knowing anyone else's personal affairs and genuinely appreciate the fact that I rarely know the specifics of the psychic messages I relay to others. I hope that this is your attitude as well. It is not ethical to use psychic abilities to pry into matters that are not your concern. You need to develop symbols of your own so that you can begin the next phase of your own psychic development.

The following is a list of some of the symbols, with their interpretations, that I receive when giving my own psychic readings. Some of these symbols may have similar interpretations to your own, but most will not. They are given as examples only.

Moving hands—actively working
Still hands—lack of work
Two buildings—change of jobs
Arrow pointing toward me—someone coming toward me
Arrow pointing away—someone leaving
Suitcases—a trip
Pine tree—a sturdy character
Books—education
Frog—jealousy
Dove—peace, harmony
Fox—slyness
Garbage can—scandal
Bell—joy, victory
Bird—coming of good news
Mountain—struggle
Candle—faith in spiritual things
Owl—spiritual wisdom
Horse—earthly wisdom
Elephant—physical strength
Rose—love, appreciation
Cross—protection
Circle—completness
Key—a new opening, or a change
Door—new situations
Stairs—an easy climb
Saucer—something left over
Ticket—entrance into something previously excluded from
Signature—binding agreement, contract
Sunflowers—interest in Indian history
Sword—interest in general history

Triangle—interest in metaphysics
Red cross—involved in medicine
Blue cross—spiritual leader
Yellow cross—philosopher or philosophy
Stapler—fasten things together
Primroses—fall season
Daffodils—springtime
Clocks—under the law of time, or something that
    is possible but not yet firmly in the future
Doll—girls
Marbles—boys

I could continue listing my own symbols, but it is important that you develop and interpret your own symbols in accordance with your experiences, your personality, and your psychological state of being.

How to Develop Your Own Symbolic Psychic Language

The first step is to list the various situations and circumstances you will need symbols for. In other words, develop symbols that would answer questions *you* might ask. The most obvious questions are those that concern work, the home, family, children, and so on, but your world is broader than that. You should include symbols denoting such things as travel, education, danger, real estate, investments, geographical changes, hidden talents, and the like. Think very carefully of the questions you might ask, then list the symbol and the subject. I'll start you out with a few subjects. You go from there. Forty different symbols will give you a very firm foundation in the pursuit of your own common-sense psychic development.

SUBJECT	SYMBOL
1. Work	_____
2. Children	_____
3. Education	_____
4. Health	_____
5. A sale	_____
6. A move	_____
7. Prosperity	_____
8. Summer	_____
9. Winter	_____
10. January	_____
11. February	_____
12. March	_____
13. Danger	_____
14. A trip	_____
15. Eastern states	_____
16. Southern states	_____

SUBJECT	SYMBOL
17. Various climates	_____
18. Mountains	_____
19. Ocean	_____
20. Government	_____
21. Musical talent	_____
22. A letter	_____
23. Intelligence	_____
24. Inheritance	_____
25. A physical handicap	_____
26. Love	_____
27. Marriage	_____
28. Home	_____
29. Friends	_____
30. Relatives	_____
31. _____	_____
32. _____	_____

SUBJECT	SYMBOL
33. _____	_____
34. _____	_____
35. _____	_____
36. _____	_____
37. _____	_____
38. _____	_____
39. _____	_____
40. _____	_____

You must now memorize this list of forty subjects and the symbol that belongs to each. And you must not only memorize them. You must program your subconscious mind as well.

Programming the Subconscious Mind

Programming the subconscious is an easy task if it is done on a daily basis. During this week, every day, tell your subconscious mind, as an example, that every time you are to give a message concerning a work vibration that you will clairvoyantly see [whatever your symbol for work may be]. Go through the entire list in this manner.

You must be faithful to this exercise until your symbols and their meaning are firmly implanted in your subconscious mind. This is the psychic language that will enable you to give readings concerning the past, the present, and the future.

Clairvoyance Is Not Always Symbolic

For most of this chapter I've emphasized the symbolic nature of your clairvoyant vision, and now I'm saying that all visions are not symbolic in nature. As you progress through this program, that statement will seem less contradictory than it does now. "Literal clairvoyance" usually occurs only when you give readings by means of psychometry (see chapter four). But because each of us is one of a kind, there may be some difficulty in differentiating literal-symbolic clairvoyant vision. The only way that you can be sure that a message is symbolic rather than literal is by trial and error. It won't take long for you to discover the difference between the two. You will never reach perfection in your psychic work. I've been giving readings for over two decades, and believe me, there are times I've really goofed up a reading. I say *I* because our psychic impressions are always 100 percent correct. Error occurs in the reader's interpretation of the impression.

This is a point I'd like to illustrate with some predictions I gave on New Year's Eve, for events that were to occur during the coming year. One of the two very good psychic impressions I received I interpreted correctly, the other I did not.

I saw a triangle with "IBM" written at each corner. A man was standing at the peak of the triangle, but suddenly he disappeared. As the man vanished, I felt crushing chest pains. My prediction? "There's going to be a change at the top of one of the greatest computer companies in the United States. Someone has chest pains and leaves. I'm talking about IBM."

The following June, Thomas Watson, IBM's chairman of the board, resigned after having a heart attack.

Another time I saw the State of California as a map. San Jose was marked with a star. As I looked at the map, I felt myself being drawn southwest, toward Santa Barbara. I then saw the star that marked San Jose on the map shoot into the air. I told the assembly: "I see a new star rising. It looks to be between San Jose and Santa Barbara. It could be a person—no, it's astronomical."

The next month, the newspapers carried a story concerning the first successful photography of a peculiar kind of star—a pulsar. The article noted that this pulsar was generally called the "southwest composition." This great "first" occurred at San Jose's Lick Observatory.

Notice that I said, "I feel myself being drawn southwest, toward Santa Barbara." Here was an error. Santa Barbara had nothing to do with the prophecy—it was the *southwest feeling* that did. The newspaper article referred to the "southwest composition." My prediction should have concluded, "There is something concerning the southwest."

Although I did err, it was a good prophecy. And the same will be true with you. Don't panic and don't feel inferior just because you make an error. But to build your self-esteem, try following this advice for a while.

If you encounter a new symbol or a new feeling while giving a reading, describe aloud what you are seeing or feeling. This is especially true when giving another individual a reading. The symbol and/or feeling may not mean a thing to you, but it could mean a great deal to the person that you're reading for.

One evening a lady, whom I had never seen before, asked me to give her a very brief reading. I closed my eyes and saw myself standing on a stage as the opera

Madame Butterfly was being performed. The aria "One Fine Day" was being sung. I told the lady exactly what I saw and heard because I could not interpret its meaning. Fortunately I didn't try; I was receiving a "literal vision" and not a symbolic one. I didn't know it was literal, but I should have. The clue that I was receiving a literal vision should have been evident: I saw none of the familiar symbols that usually come to me clairvoyantly.

The lady in question had just come from an audition—in which she had sung the particular aria I had heard clairaudiently. Because my vision placed me on the stage during the opera, it obviously meant that she would be chosen to sing the role—and she was.

If I had attempted to interpret this psychic impression I would have messed it up beyond recognition. Whenever *you* are faced with clairvoyant scenes, clairaudient sounds, or clairsentient feelings that are unfamiliar, look for their literal meanings. If your vision is symbolic and in need of interpretation, you will notice the appearance of familiar symbols in your vision.

Now some practice. Below are three symbols. Let's pretend that you have seen these symbols clairvoyantly, in the exact order shown.

What could this mean? This is my reading: "There will be a scandal around two people you look up to. Nothing will come of it, however, because I see peace and harmony prevailing."

In past examples I've referred to the pine tree as signifying a "sturdy character" or a "person." I didn't mention whether the person was a man or a woman. Here's a method you can use to determine the gender of your symbols (if appropriate).

There are some people who instinctively know if they are reading for, or about, a male or female. But most individuals need a little practice in making this determination—a little practice in training themselves to *feel in a specific way.*

Your subconscious mind is very receptive to conscious, repetitive suggestion. In my psychic classes I teach that male vibrations should be felt from the right and female vibrations from the left, and it has proven to be very effective. Your role in this exercise is simply this. Tell your subconscious mind, "I will feel male vibrations from the right. I will feel female vibrations from the left." Over and over again you must tell your subconscious mind how you are going to respond to this feeling. It won't take a great deal of time before your subconscious mind responds as you direct, but it is a matter of practice—crucial practice. This determination of gender is vital information that you need not only in the present learning process, but in all your future psychic work as well.

"Quickies" Often Lead to Error

Unless you choose to treat your psychic development as a private, confidential matter, great demands will be put upon your time and talents. And under the pressure of time, there is the inclination to toss off a "quickie reading." Unless you are terribly good at it, this will most often result in either an erroneous message or one that just does not make sense. A former student of mine had an interesting experience that illustrates just what can happen to a psychic impression when you're pressed for time.

Phil was in Oregon giving psychic demonstrations.

He had spent the entire afternoon reading billets and auras and doing readings via psychometry. At the end of the day he was tired and anxious to leave the auditorium. As always happens, a group of people were waiting to ask "just one more question." Phil glanced at a lady and closed his eyes as he looked at his clairvoyant picture. He saw a man standing very casually, almost at parade rest. His back was toward Phil. In the man's hands, which were behind his back, Phil saw a paper airplane with an arrow on its side.

Phil was in a hurry and tossed out a quick message. He said, "There is something going straight ahead, and it is going ahead without any great difficulty." This he deduced from the paper airplane with the arrow on its side. The lady said, "That doesn't answer my question. Will you describe your vision?" Phil now related the details of the image, including the fact that the man who looked to be standing so casually was in a place that looked like beach or ocean frontage of some type.

The lady for whom the reading was being given had lost her husband in an airplane crash at Coos Bay, Oregon. The question that she earnestly wanted answered was, "How did it happen?" Phil had received the answer to the question, but in his rush to leave, he had neglected to verbalize it.

The husband, the airplane, and the ocean or bay were immediately picked up by Phil. The casual stance of the man in the vision showed that the accident was the result of his own negligence and casual attitude. The accident was not, as the woman had believed, due to sabotage.

I repeat my point: If your clairvoyant picture is anything out of the ordinary for *you,* tell the person exactly what you are seeing. Let him or her interpret the message.

Individual Exercise

Take time each day to familiarize yourself with your symbols. If you neglect this exercise you might as well just lay this book aside. You cannot become a top-notch, accurate psychic if you do not thoroughly understand symbols—especially *your* symbols.

In addition to memorizing your symbols, assiduously practice seeing your symbols clairvoyantly. As you sit relaxed, say, "I want to see the symbol for work. I want to see the symbol for lack of work. I want to see a symbol for vacation," and so on. Go over each symbol from your list until it can be visualized clearly.

This exercise trains your conscious mind to respond quickly to the psychic impressions that are received from your subconscious mind. You have received psychic impressions since birth. The majority of these impressions stayed locked within your subconscious mind because we train ourselves to consciously reject what appear to be fantasy or imagination. You are now reversing this process so that your conscious mind responds to these impressions by building an image and creating a sound and/or feeling.

Group Exercises

At the beginning of your group meeting, ask the members to consult their notes from the last class session, concerning the picture(s) that were given to them during the clairvoyance exercise. Now the pictures can be interpreted. You'll be happily startled to discover the accuracy of the readings that were given by your beginner's group.

A great deal of excitement will be generated during the first half of your class. It will be difficult to keep your group from spending the remainder of the evening in giving messages. Take a break and insist that the second half of your meeting be devoted to a work session.

Begin the second half of your meeting by asking another person (say, Jane), "What symbol or symbols would you see to describe a change of jobs?" Jane might respond by saying, "I see a man clearing off a desk in one office and moving to another."

Jane would then ask a question. "My question is to Ernie. What symbols would you see if you were receiving a message about a trip to Philadelphia?"

Ernie might reply, "I see an airplane landing. . . . and in the distance I see the Liberty Bell," or, "I see an automobile traveling to the east. I see *Philadelphia* on the license plate."

Ernie would then ask Sam a question: "What symbol would you see to describe autumn?" Sam's reply could be: "I see the leaves on the trees changing colors." Or Sam may have simply heard the word *fall*, or any of a hundred different symbols or sounds.

Take turns asking questions such as those. It's excellent training, and it does illustrate the variety of symbols used by different people to describe the same thing, *but in their personal psychic language*. A great deal of your psychic learning will come from fellow group members.

I can't exaggerate the importance of this lesson. Put your whole heart into this one. You won't regret it!

DO NOT CONTINUE WITH
THE NEXT CHAPTER UNTIL
YOU HAVE DONE THE INDIVIDUAL
EXERCISES FOR ONE WEEK.

4

LESSON 4

How Psychometry Expands Your ESP

You've learned that vibrations are everything. You practiced *feeling* things in a psychic way. You have developed clairaudience, clairvoyance, and clairsentience. You know the psychic language of symbols. Psychometry is a psychic experience that utilizes every technique you've learned in the previous lessons.

What is Psychometry?

Psychometry is the divination of facts that surround an object in an invisible manner. Divination of these facts is accomplished by allowing the vibrations of an object to create a clairvoyant, clairsentient, or clairaudient reaction in your conscious mind. Whether you are aware of it or not, you have been reacting to psychometry vibrations every day of your life.

It would be very unusual if you were to go through any twenty-four-hour period without experiencing a feeling about some object, place, or person. These feelings are psychometry.

Psychometry allows you to know past or present facts concerning an object, or general feelings about that object. Everything within the universe does have a character of its own. The character of inanimate objects is determined by their environment, created by the persons who are, or were, close to the object emotionally, physically, or both. Thus, the character of an inanimate object is usually determined by its owner, the object absorbing the thoughts and feelings of its possessor. Essentially, you read the "soul" or "character" of an object.

You *cannot* give prophecies concerning future events by the psychometric method. It is quite true that you may receive information during a psychometry reading that is precognitive in nature, but this information is not received through psychometric vibrations. It is received as an "independent reading," which will be covered in chapter five.

Within the psychic field, *psychometry* has become a very misused word. Many psychics give psychic impressions or readings concerning future events by touching or holding an object belonging to an individual. They say that they are "psychometrizing" the object—using the word *psychometry* to cover any type of psychic reading involving a personal effect. This is not correct.

In this book, I use the word *psychometry* in its original and correct sense. It would be advantageous for you to do the same. It is difficult to have confidence in a psychic reading given by an individual who is unable to use correctly the terminology of his or her own field.

Psychometry is an unusual psychic experience. It sometimes, but not always, produces feelings that do not occur in other forms of psychic phenomena. Holding an object may make you feel light-headed, almost dizzy, if it belonged to a person now deceased. Don't become overly concerned if you experience new or unusual feelings during psychometry. This will soon become second nature and not seem unusual at all. There is absolutely no reason to feel any fear during your psychic endeavors—just remember that every psychic sensation is perfectly natural.

Psychometry Can Pay Very Satisfactory Dividends

Before beginning your own exercises with psychometry, I'll share some true case histories so that you will become familiar with the practical benefits of psychometry. You should know what *you* can expect when using this psychic ability.

How many times have you entered an older home and said, "I'll bet this house really has a history?" How many times have you rummaged through the attic and found personal items that belonged to your ancestors? You may have wondered what the ancestor was really like, why they had this particular object, or where the object originally came from. Psychometry is the method by which you can discover the answers to these questions about times long past.

PSYCHOMETRY IN ACTION

A lady recently gave me a very good example of psychometry in action. She's extremely good at it, although she doesn't even know what it is. She explains that she "just has 'feelings' about things."

As an amateur collector with no previous experience of antiques, this lady had been repeatedly swindled by unethical antiques dealers. She innocently paid the asking price of many an item based only on the say-so of the salesman. When she later had her collection appraised for insurance purposes she was shocked to learn that most of her purchases had little monetary value. In fact, many of her "antiques" proved to be very new reproductions of very old originals. No, she did not give up her hobby because of some bad experiences. But what she did do was spend more time making her decisions before buying. And by taking this extra time, the lady, without conscious effort, began to use her psychometric ability.

She would become fidgety. She would rub her fingers back and forth over the object she was considering buying. "Suddenly," she told me, "I could feel if it was old or not." She continued: "My husband thinks I'm crazy, but I haven't been cheated since I began having these *feelings*." I asked her to explain these peculiar feelings.

"I can't explain them," she said. "It all happens when I'm rubbing my hand on the furniture. I imagine that I see a lady's dress. It's the style and type of dress I see in my imagination that tells me to what period the furniture belongs. I know that it sounds eccentric, but I haven't been disappointed since I began imagining that I could see those period costumes."

This story may seem to have little importance in the larger scheme of things, but its resolution was very important to the woman who was being taken advantage of. It hurt her pocketbook and her pride. Psychometry restored harmony to her life, and it protected her dollars.

Psychometric vibrations can come to you through many types of objects. The thing from which you receive your psychic impressions can be a piece of jewelry, a book, a piece of furniture, a room in a house, or the entire house. In other words, vibrations can come to you from any object or any group of objects.

A Typical Reading by Psychometry

My own first experience with a professional psychometrist, of which I have total recall, occurred when I was fourteen years old. A school chum invited me to his home to witness the talents of a psychometrist who was visiting his home. I had in my possession a ring that had belonged to my mother's aunt. Because of the age of the ring, it seemed to be a suitable object for the demonstration. The psychometrist did not know me, nor was there any person present who could have any previous knowledge of the ring or its original owner.

I have listed in order what the psychic said.

1. "I feel very damp."
2. "I see two bridges."
3. "I see a rickshaw."
4. I feel violence or an accident. I feel as if I'm being thrown to the ground."
5. "I see the year 1935 written before me."
6. "I see a sign on a hotel. I can't read the sign, but I do see the letter 'G' prominently displayed."

The reading was excellent. Allow me to explain the reading, point by point.

1. *I feel very damp.* My great-aunt lived in San Francisco prior to her death. "The city on the

Bay," with its frequent fog, does often feel very damp.

2. *I see two bridges.* Two of the world's most famous and beautiful bridges are the Golden Gate bridge and the San Francisco–Oakland Bay bridge—the two bridges that link San Francisco to other Bay Area cities.

2. *I see a rickshaw.* Some of my most brilliant memories of my one visit to this aunt were our frequent excursions to Chinatown.

4. *I see violence or an accident. I feel as if I'm being thrown to the ground.* I was not aware of any violence or accidents harming my great-aunt. I was, however, very much aware that she escaped unharmed from a collapsing building during the earthquake of 1906.

5. *I see the year 1935 written before me.* This meant nothing to me at that moment. Upon questioning other members of the family later, I found that her husband had died in that year. The ring had been a birthday gift from him to my great-aunt.

6. *I see a sign on a hotel. I can't read the sign, but I do see the letter "G" prominently displayed.* The message concerning the hotel sign with the letter "G" on it was exceptional. My great-aunt owned and built hotels. The last hotel she built was the St. George—named after my grandfather and her brother, both named George.

It is obvious from this one reading that the soul can remain around and within an object. That this soul, or vibration, can be picked up decades later has been proved time and again.

The Case of the Black Pentacle

I refer to this case history as an illustration of psychometry with a variation. This story concerns an object that was not in my physical presence and yet I psychically reached out and touched its vibration. You may have similar experiences.

The incident began at a meeting at which I was giving psychic demonstrations. Before I began the demonstration I clairvoyantly saw the picture of a pentacle (a five-pointed star). The pentacle was black. The clairvoyant impression made me extremely nervous and left me with a very negative feeling. I pushed the picture from my mind until I began reading for a lady in the audience. The black pentacle was from her vibration! I asked the woman if this pentacle meant anything to her. She replied with an emphatic no. Ordinarily I would have dropped the subject, but my instinct was pushing me to pursue the matter.

"Are you absolutely positive that you don't know what I'm talking about?" I asked. "It doesn't mean a thing to me," she answered, "but my son found one today and hung it on his bedroom wall."

(Here is a classic example of how a person will deny a psychic impression even though it is accurate. The lady felt that she had given an honest answer. She felt the pentacle concerned her son and not herself. This type of incident can truly upset a newcomer to the psychic world. My advice? Don't become upset every time someone denies one of your psychic impressions. The chances are that you are absolutely correct. The hang-up is with the party receiving your psychic information.)

Quite honestly, I felt that this lady was deliberately giving me a difficult time, and it irritated me. Rather than go into any depth, I simply said, "You'd better get rid of that pentacle or you'll regret it," and moved on to the next person. When she approached me after the meeting and demanded an expansion and clarification of my psychic impression I told her she could do her own investigation of the matter. (My opinion, it should be obvious by now, is that a psychic is doing a person a favor by reading for them, and not the other way around. Unless you have a specific reason for giving public demonstrations, I strongly suggest that you use your psychic abilities to enrich your own personal life.) But back to the black pentacle. The lady did do her own investigation and told me about it when I saw her a month later.

It seems that the woman was as irritated with me as I was with her on the night of the initial reading. She totally disregarded my warning of negativity—at least for about a week. Her normally straight son began to undergo a drastic personality change. He became belligerent and moody. He resorted to petty thievery. The mother was still not willing to accept that the pentacle could have such an impact on her son, but she did ask the boy where he had gotten it.

The son had helped some neighbors haul trash to the dump. In the debris he spotted the pentacle, liked it, and kept it. Now the mother took the medallion to the neighbor's home to ask about its origin.

The man of the house was reluctant to speak of the pentacle. After a great deal of persuasion he told her that the pentacle had belonged to his mother-in-law, who was now in a mental institution. According to the son-in-law, the woman had had mental problems for some time, but shortly before she was committed she had begun to practice "black magic." She used the pentacle in a ritual to place curses on people.

The boy's mother drove to a deserted stretch of cliffs above the Pacific Ocean and tossed the pentacle as far out to sea as she was able. Within a few days, her son returned to normal.

The son had unconsciously attuned himself to the negative "soul" of the pentacle. When the pentacle was removed from his sight he unconsciously cut the negative vibration. How would traditional psychiatry handle the problem? Poorly! Fortunately, however, there are many nontraditional psychologists who are very familiar with the importance of the psychic world around us.

Practical Psychometry

Under ordinary circumstances you are probably quite happy to go to new places and to meet new people. But there are days that, "for some reason," you just do not feel right about going to a certain place, or you just do not want to meet certain people. It's a feeling you cannot express adequately in words. If you do go after experiencing these feelings you probably return home saying, "I knew I shouldn't have gone there!"

These uneasy feelings do not always denote "negativity." They may simply indicate a lack of rapport. I have met some very nice people whom I simply could not stand being around. There was not a thing wrong with them, and there wasn't with me. We just were not on the same "wavelength." If you pay attention to your feelings and don't get hung up on *why* you feel as you do, you will rarely find yourself in an uncomfortable or unpleasant environment. Using psychometry in this simple manner can *add* a great deal of peace and harmony to your daily life.

HOUSES AND HOMES ALWAYS EXPRESS THEIR "SOUL"

When I was sixteen, I was working for a youth group in the renovation of a large mountain home that was to be a summer camp for underprivileged children. It was a large house with many rooms. Except for cooking utensils, the house was relatively bare of furniture.

We had arrived late in the afternoon and were not to begin work on the house until the next morning. I found a rocking chair and decided to take a short nap.

I had not sat in the chair for more than thirty seconds when I began to feel very, very ill. I was faint and experiencing a great deal of pain. My first thought was to get a drink of water. It was by willpower alone that I managed to make it to the kitchen. But instead of finding relief, I began hearing the voices of women speaking in a foreign language. There was a great deal of laughter. I got outside as quickly as possible. As soon as the fresh air hit my face I felt perfectly normal. I believed that I had drifted off to sleep and not quite awakened from a dream.

A few minutes later I re-entered the house and, feeling no unusual sensations, I began looking over the remainder of this very beautiful home. I had a very calm and peaceful feeling until I entered a room that had been the study or library. I felt instant irritation. I felt uncomfortable and unwelcome. I never entered that particular room again.

Later in the evening we built a fire in the large fireplace and enjoyed its warmth while sitting on the benches that had been built for that purpose. I suddenly felt very lonely and depressed. Tears began to well up in my eyes. Quickly excusing myself, I fled to the bedroom that had been assigned to me. When I closed the door behind me, I immediately felt happy— almost elated.

Several days later I went to a small grocery store in the nearest town. When the very friendly proprietor learned that I was working at the new camp, he told me about the house and its previous occupants.

The owners of the home had been a retired physician and his wife. The house was built to be very similar to the home they had left in their native Switzerland. This house had been the scene of large family gatherings, and the neighbors were always invited. The grocery store owner said, "I wished that I could speak German. The women were always in the kitchen working and laughing. I always wondered what they were laughing about." (These were the voices I had heard in the kitchen on my first day at the house.)

"Doc was an eccentric person," the grocer said. "His house was open to all. He encouraged everyone to make themselves at home; but no one was ever allowed to enter his study. He wouldn't even let his wife in the room to clean it." (The origin of my own unwelcome feeling when I had entered the study.)

"One day," the grocer continued, "Doc's wife found him dead in his rocking chair. He had had a heart attack." (The dizziness and pain I had experienced when I sat in the same chair.) He told me of the depth of the widow's sorrow. "Every night she would sit by the fireplace, where they had always sat together. She would cry until she became hysterical." (My sorrow as I sat on these same benches.)

I was very young and I was not consciously trying to feel the character of the house, and yet the "soul" of the house was brought to me very strongly. Why? A rapport that I cannot explain existed between me and the vibrations from this mountain home. At that point I did not have the experience to know that all I had to do was to "turn the feelings off" if I didn't like what I was feeling.

THE PSYCHOMETRIC HOUSE, PART II

A friend had become very unhappy with his wife during the course of house hunting. After a great deal of searching, they had finally found a house that was the right size at a price they could afford. "But," he said, "I think my wife is nuts! She won't buy the house because it makes her nervous. Can you believe that?" he asked. "The house makes her nervous!" Yes, I did believe it.

My friend was fortunate that he had such a psychic wife. His wife was feeling the character of the house. It did not match her personality. If she had moved into the house she would have become even more nervous and irritable—and her husband in turn.

I was acquainted with the realtor who was trying to sell the house and asked her about its previous occupants. It was for sale because of a very bitter divorce proceeding. It is obvious that the house was expressing the character of its previous occupants.

The same realtor uses psychometry to very practical ends. "When showing prospective buyers a house," she said, "I always tell them to look around while I wait outside. I tell them to relax and look around—'Make sure that the house *feels* like your house before you make up your mind.'" If they have any strange feelings or hesitancy, she tells them, "This must not be the house for you. There's a right house for everyone and we'll keep looking until we find it." She's made many people happy. As a bonus, she's also made a great deal of money.

Psychometry and Law Enforcement

It is no longer unusual to read of a police department requesting the help of a psychic to aid in a murder investigation, but the majority of times psychics help are still not publicized—for some very practical reasons. Psychics don't want to become part of the statistics themselves.

Professional psychics who devote themselves solely to this type of investigation can be placed in a great deal of danger if knowledge of their contribution becomes public. In the criminal's mind it just might seem logical to murder a second person—especially if it seems that person can "point the finger" at them.

Psychics are usually at their best during murder investigations. A psychic is able to stand in the vicinity of a murder, touch various objects in close proximity of the crime, and describe the crime along with a physical description of the murderer and other clues. One reason for the high level of success is that a great deal of emotion is always expended just prior to a murder.

Murder isn't the only reason for law enforcement agencies to enlist the help of a psychic, but that use is most similar to what you'll learn in this lesson. Psychometry requires physical contact with an object(s), just like those associated with such a crime.

There are many psychics throughout the United States who devote their time exclusively to locating missing children—and, yes, missing pets as well.

In many department stories, specialty shops, and manufacturing companies, theft by employees is widespread. Most often the item stolen is first concealed somewhere on the premises until an opportunity arrives to safely move the object from the building. If security personnel or management discover the hidden merchandise before it is taken from the building, how can they find out who the thief is? Through psychometry, of course.

Association and Psychic Development

In addition to the psychic language of symbols, which you've previously learned, it's often overlooked that people you know may also be symbolic in your psychic world. This is termed "psychic association." Let me give you an example.

I'm acquainted with a man whose most salient characteristic is sales ability. He's a real go-getter and can achieve almost anything he sets his mind to. He is quiet, but mentally as strong as a bull. His placid exterior conceals a fearless nature that goes unobserved until a person has grappled with him in a business venture.

Whenever I am giving a psychic reading and either have a vision or think of this man, I know that the person I am reading for, or about, has these same characteristics. By just thinking of this man, I can give quite a long, convincing, psychic demonstration. If *you* see, hear, or think of a person familiar to you in the midst of a psychic impression, be aware that you are receiving valuable psychic information.

Use Your Voice to Speed Your Development

Psychic impressions are subtle. They sometimes need to be helped along. Your most valuable tool in strengthening your impressions is the sound of your own voice. The sounds of speech are vibrations. When you are working with psychometry (the vibrations around an object), your own voice does much to put you on the same wavelength as that of your psychometry vibration.

In my classes, a main point is that my students must keep their mouths moving—even if it is to talk about the weather. By talking of things not even associated with the object at hand, the student gradually begins to feel drawn into the vibration of the object. Suddenly, legitimate psychic impressions are possible.

There is an additional reason for talking: You need the attention of the group. Nothing is more boring than

to sit watching a psychic clutch an object in silence as
the minutes tick by. Boredom can totally destroy a
psychic impression. Learn this from the very beginning: Speak quickly and give your message. Don't
waste everyone's time by using ten minutes to give
information that can be given in one minute or less.

Group Exercises

Before your group meets, tell each member to bring
small objects to the meeting—especially those that are
old or associated with events of emotion. The objects
could be a ring, a pipe, a book, or an impersonal item
such as a vase. As the members enter the room, have
them place their objects in a covered box so that no
one is aware of which article belongs to whom.

After the group is seated and at ease, have each
member select an object from the box. Begin the psychometry reading in this manner:

1. If possible, hold the object between the palms
   of the hand. If you feel like rubbing the object,
   do so.
2. Close your eyes for better concentration.
3. Immediately begin talking—even if at the beginning you feel that you are making no sense.
4. Without dwelling on interpretations, give out
   with what you feel, what you think, and what
   you hear.

If I experience difficulty in getting myself going at
psychometry demonstrations, I ask myself quick mental questions. I ask, "What do I feel?" I immediately
verbalize my feelings. I then ask such questions as
what I see, what I hear, and so on. I then ask who owns
the object. If time permits, I discuss the validity of the

reading. Follow the same procedure in your group meeting.

One of the greatest obstacles to overcome in all of psychic development is the fear of being wrong. No one is always right, and you shouldn't expect to be. You may also feel a sense of disappointment if your impressions are very short. Remember that it is quality, not quantity, that really matters.

A student recently had this fact brought home. A man asked the student if he would hold a billfold. The student was very disappointed when he received only three things.

He said, "I feel cold. I feel as if I'm falling. I hear the name Dan."

The student then apologized for failing to give "a good reading." He shouldn't have apologized. The billfold had belonged to the man's son, Daniel. He had been killed in a helicopter crash in a snowstorm. The man was testing the student. He began a skeptic, but became a convert.

As your group gives their psychometry readings you'll hear such comments as, "I feel so foolish," "I'm embarrassed," "I'm imagining things." Don't dwell on those statements. Keep the group talking. The feelings of pessimism will soon be replaced by shouts of "I didn't think I could do it!"

To be honest, you must push yourself to the hilt when learning psychometry. Don't expect to be perfect the first time—or the second time, for that matter. Just do your best.

There are some people who are exceptionally good at psychometry from the very beginning, and there are those who have to do a great deal of practicing. This doesn't mean that the mediocre beginner will never surpass someone who's the first one out of the gate.

I recently had a student who, for the first two or

three weeks, seemed a hopeless cause. I drew her aside and explained that her feelings of inferiority and her natural shyness were holding her back. I insisted that she get up before the group and begin talking whether she believed what she was saying made sense or not. By the end of the seventh week, my slow starter was the star pupil.

During all of the psychic development classes I've taught over the years, I've looked for the reason why some people are better at psychometry than others. The only thing I've found is that those people who use the practical side of their brain more than the creative side do less well in psychometry.

Problems That May Occur

I'm not going to deceive you in any way by saying no one has problems with psychometry. They do! But it's not because their ESP is failing them. *Physical* circumstances can create the problem. I'll use one of my own experiences as an example.

My grandmother never went anywhere without carrying a small silver shield that said GRAND ARMY OF THE REPUBLIC across its face. The shield belonged to her father who, after the Civil War, marched in every patriotic parade. The emblem was pinned to a sash that Union veterans wore during these parades.

One day, quite unexpectedly, my grandmother asked me to give a psychometry reading on the shield. Her sister had stopped by for coffee. Of course she wanted to hear the reading; he had been her father as well as my grandmother's.

As soon as I held the shield, I began talking very rapidly. I was receiving so much information, I just couldn't get all of it expressed. A great deal of the information was very personal.

When I'd finished the reading, my grandmother

said that 99 percent of what I said was incorrect—
except for what I could have knowledge of by reading
history or listening to family stories.

One thing I didn't understand was why my grandmother was so very angry. Her sister wasn't angry. She
just sat there stroking her chin. It was obvious that she
was doing some heavy thinking.

After my great-aunt had left, my grandmother and
I discussed what I had received in the reading. Everything I'd read was about her, not her father. And most
of the things I read were secrets from my grandmother's past. But I now knew why she had become so
angry at the conclusion of the reading. She said, "Kate
heard everything. In fifteen minutes every one in the
family will know about it!"

Here's what happened. The shield had belonged to
my great-grandfather, who only wore it when he was
marching in a parade. But my grandmother carried it
for years as well. Whose vibrations did I read from the
shield? My grandmother's, of course.

It's true that there were minute vibrations linger-
ing on the shield from the original owner, but they were
so dominated by my grandmother's vibrations that it
would require the use of all my psychic senses to give a
reading about my great-grandfather.

Individual Exercise

During this week, you'll need six or seven old articles—as old as you can find. If you don't have any such
articles, visit a second-hand store, garage sale, or flea
market and pick up some inexpensive items. Then:

  1. Allot fifteen minutes a day as a time to sit
     down, be quiet, and relax. Keep a pad and
     pencil handy so that you can make notes of
     your impressions.

2. Hold an object between your palms and mentally ask, "What do I feel?" Write down your feelings.
3. Next, ask, "What do I see?" Note your clairvoyant experience.
4. Finally, ask, "What do I hear?" Write it down.

At the completion of this simple exercise, you will have a fairly complete history of the object in question.

At the beginning of your development it helps to have the information you receive verified by others. Psychometry is an excellent psychic area in which to practice this verification.

Many of my students exchange six or seven articles among themselves during the week. At the end of the week they get together to compare notes.

Three students were recently amazed when they compared their notes. They had gone to a second-hand store and purchased three pieces of glassware and three pieces of jewelry, exchanging the articles during the week. Their notes revealed that they had given identical physical descriptions of the previous owners of the objects. Many details of their notes did vary, but the central facts of all the impressions matched completely.

PRACTICE THE EXERCISES IN
THIS CHAPTER FOR ONE WEEK
BEFORE MOVING ON TO THE NEXT
CHAPTER.

5

LESSON 5

How to Give an Independent Reading

Independent reading is the simple act of giving a psychic impression without using a physical object, as you do with reading billets or performing psychometry.

The majority of "readings" you've given in the previous lessons have been of the past and the present. During this lesson, you'll receive information in a similar way, but it will concern future events.

It's true that when giving readings concerning the future you're not going to have instant verification, but that's something you will get used to. Believe me when I say that you'll hear about it one way or the other.

How to Conduct an Independent Reading

There are so many ways to conduct independent readings that I'm only going to give a few examples. You'll get the idea right away.

Suppose you're asked to give readings at one of the "psychic fairs" that are popular all over the country. Readers usually sit in chairs scattered about a room or auditorium. A chair faces the reader, waiting for a customer. Sometimes there's a card table between the reader and customer, although its only function is to give you a place to rest your elbows on or to hold something to drink.

When I give an independent reading, my usual practice is to say to my client, "Please don't ask any questions. I'll read for you first, and if I don't answer your question, you can ask me."

Other readers prefer to have their clients ask questions first. It's easier this way, but it doesn't always appear to be on the up-and-up, though I know some very fine readers who do their readings in this manner.

If you're giving a public demonstration before a group of people, just stand up before them and look around the room until you *feel* the person you should read for. After you've identified the person, relax and start talking. Finish that reading and immediately move on to another person.

INDEPENDENT READINGS AT A DISTANCE

In the psychic world, vibrations are not limited by distance. You don't have to see the person you're reading for. It can be done over the telephone as easily as if the person is sitting next to you.

Independent Reading Can Create Unique Problems

Most psychics claim that independent reading is the easiest form of psychic communication. I have found the opposite to be true. Many of the problems confronted in this type of reading apply only to those who demonstrate their psychic abilities publicly. Even though you may use your psychic attributes privately only, you should be aware of certain considerations.

I once knew a very good psychic who had been raised in a very strict and orthodox environment. She had reached middle age before becoming aware of her psychic abilities, but her childhood experiences still colored her personality, even though *she* believed she had left the past behind her.

As a young girl, this psychic had been taught that the wearing of makeup, the coloring of a woman's hair, and so forth, were sinful. Invariably, at a public demonstration, this psychic would look around at the audience and give her first reading to women who were wearing a great deal of makeup and/or had obviously dyed their hair. All of these messages were negative— usually bringing a great deal of embarrassment to the recipients of the readings. The psychic was not intentionally slanting her messages, but she was not following one of the most basic of psychic commandments: *Thou shalt not make moral or ethical judgments about any psychic information received for an individual.*

A group of psychics (myself included) once held a "psychic fair" to help raise funds for the building of a new church (to which none of us belonged). We had a packed house and raised a good deal of money—but we all agreed that it was the most strenuous psychic day we had ever spent. The majority of people who came for the psychic readings were, putting it kindly, quite bizarre. One particular reading remains vivid in my mind.

A very attractive young woman asked me for a reading. Everything I received for the woman I found personally abhorrent. In fact, I found it very difficult to act civil toward her. It took every ounce of willpower to give the young woman a legitimate message without adding my personal opinion about her conduct. What bothered me might not have bothered you, but here's the story of the young woman.

This woman wanted to have many children by as many different fathers as possible. She had already had three children, with three different men, though she had never been married. Her question for me was whether she would be able to conceive a child with a married man who was her neighbor. My personal response was "I wish you wouldn't," but I kept that to myself. I simply gave her the psychic answer I received, which was "yes."

As difficult as it may be, you must not allow your opinions to color your psychic impressions. This is the greatest downfall of the psychic. It does more harm than good—not only to the psychic, but to the recipient of the message as well. It can give the individual a very legitimate excuse not to believe in you or your ESP abilities, and by extension no one else's. Your responsibility is to tell people exactly what you hear, see, or feel. Don't tell them what you think they want to hear unless it's a legitimate psychic impression. You're probably wondering why I'm even bothering to give you this advice. You will, however, discover for yourself that it's very difficult advice to follow.

Physicians rarely treat members of their own families because it is difficult to remain objective when diagnosing or treating the illnesses of ones they love. The same principle applies to psychic readings. The tendency is to visualize things *we* want to see and ignore those things we don't want to see. "Yes," you might say, "but I want to warn them if something is going to happen to them."

If a loved one is in danger, you'll know about it without a conscious reading. Instinct, intuition, extrasensory perception, or whatever you want to call it, warns you of danger concerning a loved one. That's something we're born with—an inner urge to protect family and loved ones. What you're learning in these lessons has pushed that protective instinct into your conscious mind.

BEING LED ON

Being "led on" is another common problem for those who give public demonstrations. As you watch the individual you're reading for, you may notice certain facial expressions that lead you to believe that you're really on the wavelength. A facial expression may give every indication that what you are receiving psychically is correct, or is at least welcome news concerning the future. You may be in for a surprise. At the end of the reading you may hear, "I didn't understand a thing you were talking about."

Conversely, you may read for an individual who sits staring at you with a completely blank face. You become uneasy and unsure. But plug ahead. You just may hear that it was the most accurate reading the individual has ever received.

The moral is that you shouldn't allow yourself to be swayed by facial expressions or external appearances. In other words, don't allow yourself to be led down the wrong psychic road—many people will intentionally used varied facial expressions to test you. I am the first to admit that it takes practice to overcome these obstacles, and it isn't easy. I can remember many times that I let such a thing happen to myself. The experience can be humiliating.

Negative Messages

This goes back to a basic question: "Is the glass half full or half empty?" Any person who possesses the most elementary psychic knowledge has a moral obligation to recognize that the glass is *always* half full, never half empty. This is one of your greatest opportunities to create sunshine rather than shadows. I can think of no excuse for any psychic to give a negative message. Any psychic information can be given in a positive manner if it can be given in a negative manner. Here is an elementary example of this principle:

NEGATIVE: I see that the terrible and unhappy problems that occupy your family will soon improve.

POSITIVE: I see that great peace and harmony will soon prevail within your household.

It's the same message, but there is a difference in delivery. Why emphasize the individual's problems when you can as easily emphasize the harmony? And if you give your messages in public, there is another consideration. The negative message reveals to the audience more of the individual's personal business than the positive message does.

Questions Concerning Health

There are strict laws governing the practice of medicine in all states of the country. The physician, chiropractor, or dentist must be licensed by the state before being allowed to practice his or her healing art. Psychics are not excluded from the laws. I strongly endorse the licensing of all healing practitioners. A psychic may, and should, practice healing—that is very legal. *But a psychic may not diagnose any illness, nor may he or she prescribe any remedy for any illness.*

What do you do when you receive the inevitable psychic impressions about a person's physical condition? You must not verbalize these psychic flashes. Gently suggest that the individual have a physical checkup without alarming him or her.

You will also receive impressions of psychic cures for various illnesses. This is admittedly a touchy area where you must use good judgment. Always remember that it is against the law to give a remedy. If the individual is unknown to you, you should follow the letter of the law no matter how difficult it may be. If you are reading for a personal friend you know can be trusted, you might reveal your psychic remedy, but only after receiving a promise that the friend will first consult with his or her medical doctor. If the physician approves of your remedy, you are within the law. If the doctor does not approve of your prescription, your friend must *not* follow your psychic advice.

A Los Angeles psychic told a man who was ill that he should drink a lot of water to improve his health. A harmless prescription, right? Wrong! The man almost died. The man who followed the psychic's advice had a kidney disease that required his liquid intake to be severely limited. The psychic was taken to court and charged with "prescribing medicine without a license." He received no jail sentence, but the fine and legal fees bankrupted the psychic. In addition to the financial consequences of his act, he lost such nontangibles as the respect of friends and family.

I consistently emphasize that *no* psychic is ever 100 percent accurate. The time you may be wrong just might be the time you are diagnosing or prescribing for a health problem. Don't do it! It's a dangerous practice, and it *is* against the law. (I am aware that there are some very famous psychics who do diagnose and prescribe. I know that they get away with it, but that does not make it right.)

Messages Concerning Accidents

It is not unusual for you to receive a psychic message concerning a future accident. You are receiving this message so that the accident *can be avoided*. If the unpleasant occurrence can not be avoided, you would not receive the psychic impression in the first place. Psychic glimpses of this nature are what make it all worthwhile. Make it very clear to the individual for whom you're reading that the reason you received the message was so that the danger can be avoided. This precognition is a flag to make the person more alert to danger. Above all, don't tell someone that he or she is going to have an accident and then drop the subject. This is a terrifying experience for the individual, who will believe that the accident is unavoidable. Chances are they'll make the accident happen. *Be constructive, not destructive.*

Children and Public Demonstration

Children are naturally psychic. Children should be allowed to freely use these psychic talents—but in a wholesome manner. I have found that many parents like to tag these childhood experiences with psychic terms. This new vocabulary that the child acquires sets them apart from their peers if they use the words in their everyday associations. For the sake of the child, wait until he or she matures before telling him or her that his or her experiences may be unique. Let your children speak openly about their psychic experiences, but let them use *their* terminology. If you want a normal child, don't show any more interest in the child's psychic experiences than in any other everyday experience.

I have watched in horror as many a well-meaning

parent has cast a child into the public arena, proud of the psychic ability of the child. But I have yet to see one of these children grow up as a normal human being. Their adult lives are a disaster, plagued with emotional and psychological disorders.

A child remains a child but a little while. A child is not emotionally prepared to handle such things as Gladys is unfaithful to her husband, Fred is an alcoholic, Mike steals money from where he works, and so on. The child will learn of this kind of adult behavior when he or she is better able to handle it. The child who is overly aware of the weaknesses of the adult world can hardly be expected to respect it. Such a child will be less likely to submit to the adult discipline and rules.

Individual Exercises

This is a relatively relaxed psychic week, so take it easy. Don't get overanxious and push ahead. Your mind needs a break. Give it the rest it needs without blocking out any previously acquired information. Take your usual quiet time each day and practice your symbols (you'll never be at your psychic best without them) and add ten new symbols to your psychic language.

SUBJECT	SYMBOL
1. _____	_____
2. _____	_____
3. _____	_____
4. _____	_____

5. _____   _____

6. _____   _____

7. _____   _____

8. _____   _____

9. _____   _____

10. _____   _____

Here is another exericse that is not presently a part of your psychic program. Only perform the exercise if you feel, without any doubt, that you want to.

Think of a person who lives at a distance from you—one you seldom see. Write down what you think, feel, see, or hear about this person. Send them your psychic impressions and ask for comments. Any confirmation of future events will, of course, have to wait until the event occurs. If you don't want to mail the information, file it until you next see the person. In talking about "what's happened since I saw you last" you can confirm your impressions.

Group Exercises

Your entire group should be devoted to independent reading. Don't allow the group to wander onto other subjects.

You should begin the class by saying, "I'm going to read for [name]." When you have finished your reading, that individual should then read for another member of your group, and so on. Keep tight control of the group by watching the clock. No person should be allowed more than five minutes to give a reading. When the five-minute mark approaches, interrupt by saying, "It's time to move on." Stick to your guns on this one. Don't let bad habits get a foothold. Once started, they are very difficult to break. Lengthy readings will destroy your group meeting as you watch it disintegrate into boredom.

DO NOT MOVE TO THE
NEXT LESSON UNTIL YOU
HAVE PRACTICED THESE EXERCISES
FOR ONE WEEK.

6

LESSON 6

How to Read a Billet

A billet is a small piece of paper upon which a question is written. This paper is folded into fourths, with an identification written on the outside. The identification can be anything you think of—"XX," "Geronimo," "///"—or any type of symbol. It's best not to use your name because you don't want it recognized when you're being read for. Some other identifications can cause the reader problems. Let's say you pick up a billet that is designated "Book Lover." Your conscious mind will immediately think the question in the billet has something to do with books. But that's usually not the case. Practice and experience will get you over that hurdle, so be aware of it, but don't worry about it.

The question written on the inside of the paper is directed to the "unseen" (billets are often referred to as letters to the unseen). When a person thinks of a ques-

tion to ask on a billet, he or she sends vibrations into
the universe. The reader then filters, subconsciously,
through millions of other vibrations to grab the answer
to the question.

It isn't mandatory that a question even be written
on the inside of the billet. It can be left blank, but if it
is, the person to whom the billet belongs must concentrate on the question they want answered.

Billets are usually used during psychic demonstrations before large crowds. It is the fastest form of
psychic reading—at least it should be. The psychic
picks up a billet, reads the identification aloud to cap-
ture the attention of its orginator, gives the psychic
impression, opens the billet to see if the question was
answered, and then throws the billet away. He then
continues with the next billet. I suggest that you do not
ask to whom the billet belongs after each reading. This
ensures that people will feel free to ask personal or
confidential questions without fear of having their
identities revealed.

The billets themselves are usually collected from
the audience in a basket or a tray and placed on a table
at the front of the meeting room. The psychic reaches
into the basket and pulls a billet out at random.

Billet reading is one of my favorite forms of psychic demonstration. I find it much easier to give a
psychic reading when I don't know who I'm reading
for. I don't have to be concerned that my conscious
mind will prejudice or influence my reading. There are
instances, however, when you will immediately know
who you are reading for. You'll know if it's a person
you're acquainted with or you'll think, "I'm reading for
the woman sitting in the fourth row, third seat from the
aisle."

My wife has played a sort of game over the years.
Like everyone else, she likes to have a billet read. In
every instance but one, I've immediately known when

I have picked up her billet. I've read the identification, known it was her, and tossed the billet away without giving a reading. The one time I didn't know it belonged to her, my mind went blank. I said, "I'm sorry, but I don't receive one thing for this person," and I tossed the billet out without giving a psychic impression. You'll have similar experiences, and really, they're quite fun. I take psychic work very seriously, but I never allow this seriousness to overshadow my appreciation of humor. And I like a good joke—even during a psychic demonstration.

The Four Categories of Psychic Impressions

Man is endowed with four natures, which, taken together, comprise the whole of the human personality. Man possesses an emotional nature, a spiritual nature, a physical nature, and an intellectual nature. You can receive no psychic impression that does not touch at least one of these. *There is nothing else.*

For the purposes of these lessons, I refer to the four parts of man as affectional (the emotions), spiritual (of the spirit), intellectual (the mind), and physical (the body). Study the chart below for a moment.

AFFECTIONAL	SPIRITUAL
INTELLECTUAL	PHYSICAL

These squares have a great deal to do with your personal psychic growth. Let me give you an example of the important role these squares will play in your continued psychic evolution.

Earlier in this book I told you that a bee is, to me, the symbol of prosperity. But if I visualize the bee in a particular square, it becomes much more than a simple symbol of prosperity. If I visualize the bee in the affectional square, it means all is well in love. If I visualize the bee in the spiritual section of my psychic quadrant it means that the person for whom I'm reading is an active worker in a spiritual organization. If the bee is seen in the intellectual sector it means intellectual growth (most likely through new academic studies). If in the physical square, the bee means material prosperity. My one symbol of the bee now means four different things. This is a very simple method by which I quadrupled the symbols of my psychic language. And you will do the same thing.

Individual Exercises

Begin this week by spending your quiet time for the first couple of days just visualizing the four squares of man's nature. On the third day, practice placing your various symbols in these four areas in your subconscious vision—don't worry about seeing physical squares in your clairvoyant images. The symbols will appear, for example, in the upper right-hand section of your vision, but they will *not* be surrounded by a rectangle as in these charts.

On the fourth day, choose twelve of your symbols and do the following exercises. Write your symbol above the rectangle, and then, within each block, write what the symbol would mean if it were viewed, clairvoyantly in that section. By this simple practice with just twelve symbols, your subconscious mind will, at its own pace, begin to manifest all of your symbols in this manner. The pleasant part is that you will know the expanded interpretation of your symbols without having done conscious exercises to memorize them.

SYMBOL 1: _____

AFFECTIONAL	SPIRITUAL
_____	_____
INTELLECTUAL	PHYSICAL
_____	_____

SYMBOL 2: _____

AFFECTIONAL	SPIRITUAL
_____	_____
INTELLECTUAL	PHYSICAL
_____	_____

SYMBOL 3: _____

AFFECTIONAL	SPIRITUAL
_____	_____
INTELLECTUAL	PHYSICAL
_____	_____

SYMBOL 4: _____

AFFECTIONAL	SPIRITUAL
_____	_____
INTELLECTUAL	PHYSICAL
_____	_____

SYMBOL 5: _____

AFFECTIONAL	SPIRITUAL
_____	_____
INTELLECTUAL	PHYSICAL
_____	_____

SYMBOL 6: _____

AFFECTIONAL	SPIRITUAL
_____	_____
INTELLECTUAL	PHYSICAL
_____	_____

SYMBOL 7: _____

AFFECTIONAL	SPIRITUAL
_____	_____
INTELLECTUAL	PHYSICAL
_____	_____

SYMBOL 8: _____

AFFECTIONAL	SPIRITUAL
_____	_____
INTELLECTUAL	PHYSICAL
_____	_____

SYMBOL 9: _____

AFFECTIONAL	SPIRITUAL
_____	_____
INTELLECTUAL	PHYSICAL
_____	_____

SYMBOL 10: _____

AFFECTIONAL	SPIRITUAL
_____	_____
INTELLECTUAL	PHYSICAL
_____	_____

SYMBOL 11: _____

AFFECTIONAL	SPIRITUAL
_____	_____
INTELLECTUAL	PHYSICAL
_____	_____

SYMBOL 12: _____

AFFECTIONAL	SPIRITUAL
_____	_____
INTELLECTUAL	PHYSICAL
_____	_____

From this point forward in your commonsense approach to ESP, be aware of the section in which your psychic symbol appears. This phenomenon not only quadruples your psychic symbols, it quadruples your psychic proficiency as well.

Group Exercise

When everyone has relaxed and is seated at your group meeting, pass paper and a pencil to each person present. A question may be written on the inside of the billet, or it can be left blank. When folding the billet and then writing the identification on the outside, shield the identification from your neighbors. It isn't intentional, but there is a natural tendency to want to glance at the billet of the person seated next to you. It's much easier to read if you don't know whose the billet is, so resist the temptation. When the billets have been filled out, collect them in a suitable container—a bowl, breadbasket, vase, or the like. You're now ready to commence with the billet reading.

HOW TO BEGIN YOUR GROUP EXERCISE

Assign one person to time each person as a reading is given. A maximum of five minutes for each reading should be allowed. At the end of five minutes, the timekeeper should interrupt the reading by announcing, "Time's up." Conversely, if an individual gives a very short reading, coach them to continue the reading for the five-minute duration—even if they claim to be drawing blanks.

To place the group at ease, you should begin by picking the first billet from the container. Read the identification on the outside of the billet aloud (this strengthens the psychic connection between the reader and the recipient of the message).

A typical reading might go like this: "I have a

billet with ABC as the identification. As I come into your vibration, ABC, I see busy hands. This tells me that your question concerns work. . . ."

You will receive much information during the reading. You may receive personality traits, family history, or any of a thousand bits of information. Don't hesitate to give any information that you receive. Most especially, don't be concerned that your psychic impression may be incorrect, or that it may offend someone. Both are unlikely.

Don't ask for whom you're reading until after every billet has been read. After the reading of the last billet, discuss the psychic impressions you received for others, and the psychic impressions that were received for you. One important reminder: Don't become overly serious. This attitude is as inappropriate as being overly frivolous.

UNFAMILIAR SYMBOLS

During the previous lessons, you have learned approximately two hundred symbols (including the quadrupling achieved earlier in this lesson). Two hundred symbols add up to a great deal of information, a great many words; and yet there will be at least one (probably more) member of your class who will receive symbols that are completely unfamiliar during this exercise. The only explanation I can offer is that your subconscious mind works much faster than we give it credit for. Although you're not conscious of it, your mind is building a more complete psychic language for your later use.

In one of my recent classes, a lady was reading a billet for the first time. And she was doing it quite well. Suddenly she saw an unfamiliar symbol—a clairvoyant vision of Florence Nightingale. She blurted out, "The billet I am reading belongs to a nurse." But it didn't.

Let's examine how and why this symbol appeared during this reading.

I asked the student to tell me what, besides a nurse, the symbol of Florence Nightingale could mean to her. After thinking for a few moments, the lady said, "Well, it could mean 'humanitarian.' "

The lady who wrote the billet said, " 'Humanitarian' doesn't fit me at all. I have too many problems of my own to be worried about being a humanitarian."

"Well, is your name Florence" the student asked.

"No, my name's Irene," the woman who wrote the billet replied. "And it's not Nightingale, either."

The student was stumped, but ended by saying, "The only other thing I can possibly think of is that the important symbol is 'Nightingale.' Do you have any thing to do with singing?"

That was the answer! The woman who had filled out the billet without asking a question on the inside was an accompanist and voice coach at the local university.

The student who had visualized the Florence Nightingale symbol came early to the next class.

"I thought about that symbol all week," she told me, "and I've finally figured it out. When I was a child I'd sit on my grandfather's front porch in the evening and we'd listen to the nightingales. He'd always chuckle and say, 'Do you hear that? That's Florence. Florence Nightingale.' I didn't understand his little joke, but I laughed with him.

"Later, when I was a teenager I read the usual girl's books about heroines and was deeply impressed with the story of Florence Nightingale during the Boer War. But now I want to ask you a question. Why did I see a woman as a symbol of singing rather than the nightingale bird?"

I couldn't answer the question, but I could suggest that "nightingale" had two equally strong associations in her subconscious mind and thus created a confusion. The psychic symbol she received was accurate, but her interpretation was "fuzzy." I could only suggest that in the future, she tell her subconscious mind that she was to see a nightingale bird if her psychic impression had reference to singing.

If a confusing symbol enters your psychic consciousness in the same manner as it did to my student, either create a new symbol or make sure that your conscious mind is firmly told which symbols it is to accept from the subconscious mind. But, more important, make this one fact a permanent part of your psychological being: *There is nothing supernatural about a billet. It is nothing more than a piece of paper that is used as a tool to enhance a mental contact between two individuals, nothing more.*

WHAT YOU WILL DO WHEN YOU READ A BILLET

1. You will pick up a billet, read the identification aloud, and hold the billet in your hand(s).
2. You will immediately begin talking: What do you see? What do you hear? What do you feel?
3. Open the billet and read the question (if there is one).
4. Wait until all billets have been read before discussing the reading(s).

DID YOU REALLY PAY ATTENTION?

Did you really pay attention to your symbols? Did you see the symbols at the upper right of your psychic vision? Or did you see them at the lower left?

Did you have any particular feelings as you looked at your symbols? Did you feel positive? Negative? Or did you have no emotional sensations?

Did you answer the question that was written in the billet? If not, can you think back over the psychic impression and recognize how you misinterpreted your symbols? No psychic impression is received incorrectly, but it *can* be interpreted incorrectly. Be cautious, observant, and pay attention!

SEEING

After one class, a member spoke to me as he was leaving. "I answered the question in the billet," he said, "but I said that I *saw* something that I really didn't see. I said, 'I see a large building,' but I didn't actually see anything. I just knew there was a large building. I didn't really see the building until after the billet reading, and then I saw it very clearly. I think it was all imagination."

You've probably had a similar experience. What is it that makes you, like the student, say, "I see," when you have not actually had a physical visualization? This is what happens. Your subconscious mind visualizes the picture, but for some reason it is not "flipped" into your conscious mind. At the same time you *know* (without physical observation) that you are seeing the picture—and you are. *Knowing* is just as good as seeing.

The general reason for the slow movement of psychic impressions from the subconscious to the conscious mind is simple nervousness. The student I just mentioned was able to visualize the buildings after he had completed the billet reading because he was relaxed and no longer under pressure to perform.

WHAT *NOT* TO DO DURING A BILLET READING

For one thing, just don't stand or sit there after you've picked up a billet. *Get your mouth moving.* And when I say to begin talking immediately, I don't mean that you should receive a little bit of psychic information and then stop. Wait for more information, verbalize it, and then stop again. Voice vibration strengthens your psychic impressions and brings them to the forefront of your conscious mind. If you do experience difficulty in talking, it can be overcome by using a little common sense. Here's an example of how: "As I come into your vibration I feel movement [now you're stuck, but keep talking anyway]. I don't know what the movement is—maybe it's a job, vacation, or a house move [you will now have *felt* which type of move it is]. Now I understand. You're going to make a job change. [You either feel good or negative about the vibration.] I feel very positive about this job change. It can do nothing but benefit you."

The point is that you can keep talking to draw the psychic message out of your subconscious mind. If you hesitate in your billet reading you will begin to lose your self-confidence, and you'll lose the confidence of the person who wrote the billet. And then you might as well just stop and sit down.

Other don'ts during your commonsense psychic development are: *Don't* be bashful or shy about giving psychic readings. *Don't* be concerned about what other group members think of your impressions, and *don't* begin believing that others in the group have more psychic talent than you. Lastly, *don't* develop an ego problem by erroneously believing that you have been given an exceptional psychic gift. You haven't!

I have had some students in the past who were exceptionally good at their psychic endeavors. They had good delivery and stage presence—and most have been physically attractive. They go out before the public unprepared. At the beginning of their "mission" they are quite successful. But in a short time they have all become failures, leaving a bad impression on the public about the entire psychic world. These individuals believed they had a divine mission to convert the entire world to a belief in psychic phenomena. I know it sounds ridiculous, and I know you believe that it could never happen to you. I hope it doesn't, but if you begin to entertain such thoughts in even the subtlest form, stop performing publicly before you make a fool of yourself.

DON'T ALLOW RUDENESS DURING YOUR GROUP MEETING

There are many forms of rudeness—some intentional, most just thoughtlessness. But conscious or unconscious rudeness during your group meeting can have disastrous results. The most disruptive activities are: whispering while another person is reading a billet; needless shifting back and forth in one's chair; and reading this or any other book while someone is giving a psychic impression.

Many times class or group members will become overeager, receiving psychic information on a billet that another person is reading. Receiving this psychic information is all well and good—so long as you keep the information to yourself. *Reading over* another person's message (as it is called) can make the reader feel incompetent, irritated, and/or embarrassed. None of these are necessary. *Any* person can add to a message given by another psychic—that takes no talent whatsoever. It does take talent to be the polite and considerate individual that you should be.

> DO NOT GO ON TO THE NEXT
> CHAPTER UNTIL YOU HAVE
> PERFORMED THE EXERCISES
> IN THIS LESSON
> FOR ONE WEEK.

7

LESSON 7

How to See the Human Aura

Webster's New Collegiate Dictionary's definition of an aura as "a distinctive atmosphere surrounding a given source" or "a luminous radiation" succinctly states what the human aura is. These are definitions upon which neither the psychic nor the scientist would disagree. But auras are more than succinct definitions can explain. What constitutes the character of the aura? What causes an aura to exist in the first place? The answers to these questions will be answered in this lesson.

Vibrations, which are everything, determine the character of an object. This character, or vibration, is a subtle electromagnetic force that emanates from everything in the universe. You will learn to see this electromagnetic force that produces an aura.

The aura is the basic life-force of the universe and, of itself, is clear and colorless. This life-force appears as clear water or a faint luminous glow. Objects not usually considered living—stones, water, earth—have only clear, luminous radiation surrounding them. This clearness denotes perfection, the state of inanimate objects. They exist in complete harmony with the purpose for which they were created. But man does not live in this complete harmony.

Humans, having thoughts, emotions, and, most important, free will, are not perfect. The individuality of the human expresses itself in the aura in the form of color. It is the colors reflected in the aura that allow the psychic to see and analyze the character of the object surrounded by the aura.

In reality, the aura extends into infinity, but to the "psychic eye" the aura appears to extend from the human body to a distance of two to three feet. The size of the aura varies, with the variations in size (and clarity) determined by the physical, mental, and emotional state of the individual. The aura of the person who is ill (whether in a physical, mental, or emotional sense) will be smaller than that of a healthy person.

The shape of the aura that surrounds the human body is oval (it is not simply the halo that surrounds the head area in religious paintings). Since the mind is the strongest force we possess, it is around the head area that the auric oval is widest. The aura then narrows as it reaches the lower limbs and feet.

Do Animals Have Auras?

This is the pet lover's first question, and it's a good one. Everything in the universe has an aura, but the animal's aura, that of a living creature, has a luminous radiation that is more than the clear emanation denoting perfection.

The aura of the human is multicolored. The aura of the animal which survives by instinct is yellow. Yellow, depending on its shade, denotes intelligence, psychic ability, and instinct.

You will soon be able to look at the aura of your pet and determine if it's really as smart as you think it is, or if all of its reactions are instinctive. If an animal is capable of making a conscious decision, you will see another color in their aura in addition to the "instinctive" yellow. You may be happy (or not) to discover that some animals *are* capable of making conscious decisions.

The Law of Attraction

The old saying that "like attracts like" is a fact. As you continue your study of auras, this point will be proved over and over again. There is a magnetic quality to the aura that draws like vibrations back into itself—whether these vibrations are negative or positive. Many people consider this magnetism "the law of attraction."

Even if you are not religious, you will recognize the truth of the biblical statement, "What ye sow, so shall ye reap." The meaning of this scientific as well as spiritual law is simple: You do not wait until death to receive the rewards of or punishment for your actions. They come to you now—through the magnetism of your aura. If for no other reason than that of self-preservation, you can discover the benefits that are derived from living a moral and ethical life.

Your aura is you! It shows your strengths, your weaknesses, your intellect, feelings of love or hate, your optimism—it shows all of you. The aura that surrounds your physical body at this very moment is expressing the character of the object it surrounds—you!

Humans are not consistent. This basic inconsistency is reflected in the aura, which is in a constant state of flux. Every time you think or feel, your aura changes in a degree to match the intensity of your thought or feeling. Your aura conforms to what you are at any particular moment. If, for example, I was able at this moment to step on your toes or to give you a kick in the shin, your aura would reflect a drastic change.

How many times have you been in the company of people who have made you feel wonderful? How many times have you been in the company of individuals who for no apparent reason made you feel extremely nervous? To a great extent, these feelings were aroused by the level of harmony between your auras. You feel instant rapport with people whose character (and aura) is similar to your own. You feel instant conflict with those whose auras differ greatly from your own. (This does not imply that every individual with whom you feel conflict is a "bad" person. I've met some very nice people with whom I just have nothing in common. I haven't liked them, and they haven't liked me. But that does not make us enemies. We tolerate each other.)

Have you felt that someone simply drained you dry? This most often occurs when you are in close proximity to an individual who is physically, mentally, emotionally, or spiritually depleted.

In Nature, there is a law of balance. Positive energy travels to balance and neutralize negative energy. If you are the giver and not the getter of this positive energy, you will feel depleted. Temporary depletion of energy is fine—you've helped another individual—but if the feeling persists, you must turn it off. You can only give so much energy without damaging your own welfare.

Many people falsely claim that they cannot stop the flow of positive energy once it starts (I suspect they shelter a martyr complex). You can physically remove yourself from the presence of whoever draws energy from you, or you can mentally command yourself to let no more positive energy leave your aura to balance the negativity of the other person. And that's all there is to it!

Seeing the Aura

You can see an aura with your physical eyes and maybe already have. But the aura that you see with your physical eyes is clear and luminous. The aura that you see with your psychic eyes (clairvoyantly) is a great pulsation of colors.

Seeing the aura is the easiest thing that you will accomplish during this psychic program. I have never had a student who was unable to see an aura. This week's lesson is devoted to that simple task. In the next lesson you will learn the meaning and interpretation of the aura's colors.

If you begin to see colors within the aura during this week's exercise, don't attempt to interpret their meaning. You may have preconceived ideas concerning certain colors and color combinations that are psychically incorrect. Be patient and wait until next week.

Individual Exercise

You'll need a willing friend or family member to act as your "guinea pig" during this week's exercises. You'll also need a candle.

Begin your exercise by sitting in a dimly lit room with a lighted candle. Look at the candle, but don't stare. Sit and lightly gaze at the candle flame through very relaxed and droopy eyes. As you look at the candle you will notice an aura of light surrounding the flame. It will appear much as in this drawing.

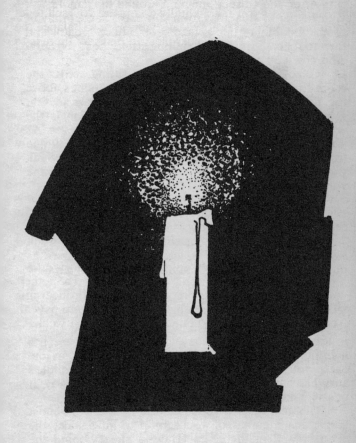

After you've seen the aura around the candle, ask your helper to sit across from you in the same dimly lit room. Ask him or her to take several deep breaths and then to relax. This deep breathing strengthens the aura. And now you must relax.

Gaze gently toward the person sitting across the room from you. Look approximately six inches above the head. Gradually you'll see what appears at first glance to be a light reflection. This reflection is the aura—and you're seeing it with your physical eyes. As you look at the aura, make a mental note of its outline (it will not be an exact oval as shown in figure 19, which was for illustrative purposes only). The aura outline will be irregular.

When you first observe the aura it may appear static, but after a few minutes you will realize that you are looking at a constantly changing, pulsating mass.

It may seem boring, but do this exercise for a full week. If possible, use as many different helpers as possible as you practice looking at the human aura.

Group Exercise

Begin your group exercise by placing a lighted candle in the middle of the room and turning off all electric lighting. As in the individual exercise for this lesson, each group member should confirm that the candle's aura has been observed. Then put the candle away. If possible, keep the room dimly lit.

The next step in your exercise is to ask the most gregarious member of your group to sit against the plainest wall in the room (Hang a sheet behind the person if your walls are decorated with many pictures or are covered with patterned wallpaper). Each member of the group should confirm that they have seen the aura surrounding the individual before continuing to the next step.

This last step in your group exercise is important, and it's fun as well. Group members will take turns describing how the aura appears to each of them. If they see colors in the aura, now is the time for them to say so. (*Do not,* however, attempt to interpret the meaning of these colors.) Hearing others describe the same aura that you have seen helps to confirm that you do not have an overly active imagination.

DO NOT GO ON TO
THE NEXT CHAPTER UNTIL
YOU HAVE DONE THE EXERCISES
FOR ONE WEEK.

8

LESSON 8

How to Analyze the Human Aura

The subject of this lesson has been the most popular in my classes throughout the years. There isn't any one reason for its popularity. Each person seems to have his or her own personal reason for liking the subject. Perhaps it's mainly the excitement produced when the student learns the many practical benefits of aura analysis.

From a teaching point of view, this is also my favorite class. I believe it results in the most practical benefits, it's the easiest to teach, and it seems the easiest to learn.

You may have started seeing colors in the exercises of the last lesson. It is in this lesson that you'll learn the meanings of those colors and their application to the understanding and analysis of human character.

Man is a very complex creature. His thoughts, feelings, beliefs, and opinions are in a constant state of change. Because of this changing personality, a valid aura analysis cannot be given at a single meeting or interview. Meaningful character analysis can only be made over a period of weeks—five or six interviews on different days of the week and varied hours throughout the day. One aura reading can give a completely erroneous picture of a person's character.

A few years ago, I was hired to teach a group of professional people who had no interest in any other psychic activity how to see and analyze the human character through the aura. I began the class by demonstrating how it was done. As I looked around the room to choose auras to read, I pointedly skipped over a woman in the first row who repeatedly raised her hand to draw my attention. She drew my attention all right; she had one of the most bitter and nasty auras I had ever seen.

At the next class, the woman was again in the front row. Instead of the negative aura I had viewed previously, I now saw the aura of an intelligent, well-balanced human being. This positive aura remained with the woman through the remainder of the classes. I later became better acquainted with the lady and told her of the terribly negative aura I had seen about her on the night of our first meeting. This woman explained to me that the first time I saw her had to have been one of the worst days of her life. She had a terrible cold. Her work wouldn't allow her to stay home in bed to nurse the virus. "Everything went wrong that day," she said. The irritation, bitterness, and nervousness I saw in her aura at our first meeting was not her true character, but I may have believed it to be so if I had not had the opportunity of seeing the woman several times after that first encounter. I would have had a completely erroneous impression—that she was an evil and vindictive woman. She wasn't. She had merely suffered through a very bad day.

The opposite occurred with a gentleman who attended one of my later classes.

The first time that I met him, I was impressed by his remarkably positive aura. It gave every indication that it reflected the inner self of a very nice, well-balanced "Mr. Nice Guy." Later meetings revealed his aura to have the coloring and vibrations of an exceptionally dangerous person. And he was. He is now in prison serving a life sentence for murder.

Before beginning the actual task of aura analysis, it's very important that you *always* keep these elementary instructions at the forefront of your consciousness:

> *Aura colors appear in much the same pattern as a rainbow. The colors closest to the body denote the individual's strongest characteristics. Those colors farthest from the body are the more minor personality traits. All clear, bright colors are positive in nature. All colors that are muddy or mixed with black signify less than perfect personality characteristics.*

Whether it is in the physical world or the psychic world, there are three primary colors—red, yellow, and blue. Any other color is a combination of the primary colors. This will be especially meaningful as you learn the meaning of each color that can be seen in the human aura. In aura analysis, the three primary colors denote specific personality traits: red the *physical,* blue the *spiritual,* and yellow *mental* characteristics.

Following is a list of various colors that can be seen clairvoyantly within the aura. It isn't necessary to immediately memorize the colors, but keep this list handy. (Although you'll learn color interpretation more quickly than you may imagine.)

RED (Physical)

Bright red   Physical strength, health, vigor. Also shows a gregarious personality.

Bright red (mixed) Anger ("I was so angry I could see red!")

Pure crimson   Love

Dark crimson   Lust, sensuality. (This color may be present in the auras of rapists.)

Rose   Seeks the good of others. Appears in the aura of social workers, nurses, ministers. I have noticed it as a very dominant color in the auras of Salvation Army workers at Christmastime.

Pink   All-around well-being. ("He's in the pink of condition!") This shows a very well-balanced, harmonious person—slow to anger, generous, and kind.

Red-orange   Salesmanship, leadership, an egocentric individual. This color shows strongly in the auras of salesmen who take their work seriously and in those of political leaders. It was very pronounced in the aura of President John Kennedy. If this red-orange color is somewhat muddy the ego takes precedence over leadership characteristics.

Red-violet   An eager participant in rituals. This person is inclined toward membership in lodges and societies.

BLUE (Spiritual)

Sky blue	True spiritual orientation.
Violet	The highest of spiritual feelings.
Very dark blue	Religious feelings that are steeped in superstition.
Blue-gray	Mental depression. ("I feel blue today!") Can also signify religious feelings ruled by fear.
Purple	Love of ceremony (as an observer rather than a participant) or of routine. Also fastidiousness, neatness, and physical cleanliness.

YELLOW (Mental)

Light yellow	Intelligence, teaching ability.
Bright yellow	An active mind.
Deep yellow	Plans, mental activity. This color is very strong around persons interested in such subjects as logic, ethics, accounting, mathematics.
Gold	Love of pure knowledge. This color dominates the aura of the religious teacher, religious philosopher, or the individual who seeks truth in all things.
Yellow-orange	Compromises, a healthy ego. This person will discuss, but never argue. They can be very persuasive, but are not inclined to dominate.

GREEN

Mixed green	Poor health. ("I feel green around the gills!")
Light green	Tolerance, love of home.
Clear green	Healing.
Forest green	Love of nature.
Dull green	Untruth, insincerity, malice.

BROWN

Clear brown	Material prosperity, industriousness.
Dull Brown	Greed, miserliness.

GRAY

Negative in all aspects, usually concerning thought.

WHITE

Pure spirit (God), the highest spiritual attainment.

BLACK

Hatred, revenge, pessimism. (Black in the aura does *not* mean death. Imminent death is not a personality trait and cannot be seen as a color within the aura. If an aura is very small and close to the body, it indicates that a person is seriously ill, but it does not mean that he or she *must* die—recovery is always possible. During the 1800s it was not unusual for a doctor or family member to consult a clairvoyant before pronouncing a person dead. Persons who were in a coma otherwise risked being buried alive.)

I have not listed every color in this table—it is practically impossible. You can make your own interpretations of additional colors by using your knowledge of the three primary colors.

Consider turquoise and aqua, both combinations of blue and yellow. In aqua, yellow is dominant. This would indicate mental prayers and mental healing. In turquoise, where blue is the dominant component, the spiritual is most outstanding. I would interpret turquoise to mean spiritual healing, with the possibility that the person with this color in the aura is a spiritual healer.

You're undoubtedly anxious to begin analyzing auras yourself. Although you clairvoyantly see the colors, you still need practice in interpretation. Let's analyze a sample aura. (When you are analyzing an aura, remember that colors *not* present in the aura can be as important as the colors that are.)

The energy field (aura) of our example is extending approximately three feet from the head. The colors listed below begin with the color seen closest to the head.

Black (6 inches)
Dull green (6 inches)
Mixed green (6 inches)

Light yellow (4 inches)
Dark blue (4 inches)
Forest green (2 inches)
Light green (1 inch)
Blue-gray (4 inches)
Clear brown (3 inches)

THE ANALYSIS

At the present time, this person is emotionally negative and bitter (black and blue-gray). In this state of mind, the person is unable to clarify problems or to look at life in a rational manner (black). This person loves nature (forest green), children, and home (light green). He is intelligent (yellow) and prosperous (clear brown). This individual's mental depression (blue-gray) is probably due to problems concerning the home and children.

Due to this man's negative attitude, his health is suffering (mixed green). It's unlikely that an improvement in health can be realized until the darkness is removed from his thinking.

There is much superstition in this man's character. He could erroneously believe that he has been placed under a curse (dark blue).

This gentleman lacks any meaningful religious experience (absence of clear blues). He is not egotistical (no orange tones). This lack of orange in the aura would indicate a serious inferiority complex. This conclusion would be reinforced by the indication of self-pity (combinations of greens).

The predominance of negative traits in this aura raises serious doubts about the person's emotional stability. This person could be easily angered—physical violence would not be out of the question. A suggestion that this person seek help from a psychiatrist or medical doctor would be appropriate.

AT THE OTHER EXTREME

For purposes of illustration, let's look at another sample aura. Its colors are pink, gold, deep yellow, and light green. The first thing to notice is the small number of colors, indicating a rather uncomplicated personality.

The next thing to note about this individual is the pink color, signifying overall well-being. The person is spiritually enlightened and loves humanity (a religious or social worker?).

This person is not burdened by financial problems—perhaps rarely thinks in a materialistic vein (absence of brown tones).

The light green denotes tolerance. (If the person were not actively involved in associations where tolerance was required, the color would not appear so strongly in the aura. The assumption would be that the person does active work with other people in some humanitarian field.)

The gold in the aura denotes a love of true knowledge (religious/moral). The deep yellow means that plans are being made—probably revolving around his or her humanitarian service.

If you were looking at an aura dominated by orange and blue tones, the indication would be that the person is involved in business and/or money-making projects.

Steps to Follow in Analyzing an Aura

Step 1 Note the colors seen in the aura in the order of size and intensity. For example:

  a. Light yellow
  b. Red-orange
  c. Deep yellow

d. Dark crimson
e. Black

(As in the rainbow, the colors within the aura overlap each other. Ignore those colors that overlap and concentrate on the colors that stand alone.)

Step 2 List the personality characteristics next to your colors.

a. Light yellow = intelligence
b. Red-orange = salesmanship, leadership
c. Deep yellow = plans, mental activity
d. Dark crimson = lust, sensuality
e. Black = hatred, revenge

Step 3 Write the analysis. My own analysis might go like this: This person is intelligent—has an active mind. He's always learning new things. (This is an assumption: An intelligent person with an active mind would almost always have the desire to keep on learning.) This person also has a strong ego. (Assumption: He has a tendency to be loud and boisterous.) This person makes plans—he doesn't allow his life to be guided by chance. He is lustful and sensual. (Assumption: The dark crimson and black indicate that sex for him has darker motives than physical pleasure. Perhaps "kinky" would be an appropriate word.) Once crossed, this man neither forgets nor forgives.

Symbols and Signatures

As you gain proficiency in reading and analyzing auras, you will note that symbols begin to appear in the aura. These symbols are not an actual part of the aura, but are rather Nature's determination that you are going to use two of your psychic abilities simultaneously. The symbols you see in the aura are prophetic messages. These symbols indicate what the individual has built into his future as a result of his or her thoughts, actions, and deeds *as of that moment*. (As thoughts and actions change, so will prophecy.)

A *signature* is a symbol that stands out in the aura in a manner unlike any other symbol seen. It is difficult to explain the difference between a symbol and a signature. But, without a doubt, you will recognize the difference between a symbol and a signature at the moment of visualization.

In the journals of English psychics, there are many references to nobility who attended psychic demonstrations incognito. These members of a royal family were immediately recognized by the signature that appeared in their auras—a crown.

A signature is a symbol that indicates a quality that is carried through a family for generations. For instance, in families with several generations of ministers, the signature of a cross may appear. In a family of philosophers, a book (depending upon the type of philosophy).

Seeing Symbols in Color

In chapter three you learned about symbols. In this chapter you've learned about colors. You've also learned how to quadruple the meanings of your symbols by dividing your clairvoyant vision into fourths (affectual, spiritual, physical, and intellectual). Through the use of color analysis, you're going to expand your symbolic psychic language even further. The symbol-color combination is very important in your increasing psychic knowledge. An illustration of this color and symbol combination is provided if you visualize a "for sale" sign that is orange in color.

The symbol (the "for sale" sign) tells you that

something is for sale. The orange color tells you if the sale will be a success or a failure. If the orange you visualize is bright and clear it would indicate a successful sale. If the orange were a murky red-orange, the sale would not be a success—probably because a very strong-willed person said no.

It is possible that the orange-colored "for sale" sign you visualized was an actual physical sign and not a symbol at all. If you are giving a reading and feel an uneasiness about the sign (in this example), verbalize what you are actually seeing and state that you're not sure whather you are visualizing a literal or a symbolic "for sale" sign.

Here's another example. My symbol of jealousy is a frog. If I see a white frog it indicates a temporary, nondamaging feeling of jealousy. A black frog indicates jealousy bordering on hate. A blue frog would denote jealousy concerning spiritual work. A yellow frog could very well indicate that the person is jealous of my psychic ability.

As is easily seen, the color-symbol combination enables you to be much more specific in your psychic pronouncements. Rather than simply saying, "I see jealousy around you," you are able to specify what, specifically, the jealousy or envy is all about.

Aura Exercises

Now it's time to practice on your own. I'll give the colors for three sample auras. You'll write the interpretation of the color next to it. Below the list, write a complete character analysis.

Sample Aura 1

Color	Interpretation
1. Pink	_____
2. Rose	_____
3. Violet	_____
4. Clear brown	_____
5. Forest green	_____

Analysis:

Sample Aura 2

1. Red-orange	_____
2. Dull green	_____
3. Dull brown	_____
4. Light green	_____

5. Light yellow   _____

6. Gray   _____

7. Purple   _____

Analysis:

Sample Aura 3

(This is a very small and dimly colored aura.)

1. Mixed green   _____

2. Deep yellow   _____

3. Red violet   _____

4. Bright red tinged with black   _____

5. Clear blue   _____

6. Light green   _____

7. Light orange   _____

8. Gold   _____

Analysis:

Aids to Aura Analysis

1. Have your subject sit against a white wall.
2. Have the room dimly lit.
3. Have the subject sit in a relaxed position without slouching.
4. Have the person sit with eyes closed, taking deep, rhythmic breaths. This deep breathing should continue for a short period only—you don't want anyone to hyperventilate.

If you experience difficulty in *seeing* the colors during this lesson, *sense* them. You can *feel* colors, you know.

Don't Forget That You Have Responsibilities

Analyzing the human aura to understand the character and personality of an individual is of inestimable value to professional counselors, doctors, social workers, psychiatrists and ministers—anyone in a position to deal with the problems or fears of a person in need. Reading character through the aura enables the psychic to give meaningful, sometimes lifesaving advice. You can help a person understand his or her own strengths and weaknesses. But there are limits to the type of advice you should give.

Unless you are trained in psychiatry or medicine, you *must* refer the individual to a properly trained professional. You can do irreparable harm to an individual if you attempt to treat, counsel, or advise courses of action in areas in which you have received no training. Seeing an aura only allows you to analyze character. *It does not make you teacher, prophet, doctor, or psychiatrist*. Use your good judgment and common sense.

Interesting Places to View the Aura

It isn't always convenient to have a person sit against a
dimly lighted wall so that you can practice viewing the
aura. Besides, that can get awfully boring. I suggest
that you find some fun places and a wide variety of
people on which to practice viewing auras. Watching
people on public transportation is fun (if you don't let
the irritation that will abound in the auras bother you).
The public library is a great place to study the aura
(especially if you want to concentrate on the yellow
tones).

Children at play make excellent subjects for analysis (a good place to view competitive instincts). If
you're not offended by a little lust, visit a singles' bar. (I
am not implying that every person who goes to a
singles' bar is lustful—but the likelihood of seeing it is
greater!) Church is another place to view a variety of
characteristics in the human aura. Ministers make
great subjects—even more interesting than the congregation.

Don't Get Off Balance

If you've followed me along to this point in the book,
you're intelligent enough to know that there is a time to
turn on and a time to turn off your psychic abilities.
Auras are fun, but don't make them so much fun that
you are constantly trying for a peek at every person's
personality.

I know a woman who jumped, panic-stricken,
from her chair during an aura class. She stumbled
about the room screaming that her eyesight had been
destroyed. (Thankfully it wasn't during one of my
classes.) The instructor caught up with the frightened
woman and shook her until she finally comprehended
that she had to "turn it off." The unfortunate woman

had become confused when she began seeing auras around every object and every person in the room simultaneously. The incident should never have happened. Remember that *you* make the determination as to what aura you will see and when you will see it.

Individual Exercises

During this week, completely familiarize yourself with the aura colors. Until the colors are memorized, learn how to look up their interpretation as quickly as possible.

Read as many auras as possible during the week— both from subjects who will sit for you for a formal personality analysis and any that you can view in an informal manner.

Group Exercises

Devote the first half of your group meeting this week to billet reading. The emphasis of these readings should be placed on the color of the symbols visualized. For purposes of practice only, the reader should say aloud what colors are seen in the symbols.

During the second half of your meeting, choose two people to sit against a light-colored wall so that the others in the group may analyze their auras. Give each person a pad and pencil to do an analysis. (Each group member should choose only *one* of the subjects to analyze, not both. Reading two auras would take too long.) Whichever subject they choose, have the members write that name at the top of their papers. Make sure you've set a time limit on the exercise.

Toward the end of the time allotted for the aura analyses, you may want to do an experiment. If you have the time, it can prove to be interesting.

First, take three pieces of paper. On the first write,

"A man kicking a dog." On the second slip write, "A gently flowing mountain stream." On the third write, "A large pink rose."

Inform your group that the analysis period is over and that you are going to do an experiment. Pass one slip of paper to the people sitting against the wall and ask them to concentrate on what's written on the paper (both individuals should concentrate on the same paper). Then ask the members of your group to write down what is now the predominant color in the aura. Do the same thing with the second and third pieces of paper.

Many people are embarrassed about giving an aura analysis. They believe that what they see may not be what the subject wants to hear. To overcome this sense of uneasiness, collect all of the group's aura analyses and mix them up. Pass them out again, making sure that no individual has the aura and analysis that he or she wrote. Each person should read aloud that analysis.

Before the group disperses for the evening, allow your "guinea pigs" to defend themselves—either agreeing or disagreeing with what others saw as their dominant personality characteristics.

PART

III

9

The Importance of Dreams in Psychic Phenomena

Dreams can be an important part of *ESP for Everyone* if *you* choose to make them so. The lessons in this book were primarily concerned with the conscious acceptance of psychic impressions.

Many people choose not to consider dreams a part of their psychic development. In many instances these same people have read dream books. They've discovered that interpretation of dreams in accordance with the books' instructions have been completely erroneous.

Dreams are symbolic. A dream book is no more valid than if you were handed a book with instructions to "interpret every one of your clairvoyant symbols according to this book." Whether the receiver is in a conscious or unconscious state, symbols do not mean the same thing to every person.

Another objection to dreams concerns trust. Many people just do not trust unconscious psychic impulses. But try for a few moments to forget all of your past objections to dreams as valid psychic phenomena. Read on.

In the Beginning

When man was created he was given five physical senses so that he might perceive and understand the physical world in which he had been placed. In addition to the physical senses, man was given psychic senses so that he might survive in the world. And in addition to the two forms of senses, man was given a spirit. Spirit is man's eternal self.

In the waking state, the physical senses dominate the spirit. It is in the sleep state that the spirit is the dominant element. It is only during sleep that the spirit can be fully free to accept inspiration. Inspiration and precognitive visions are expressed in our dreams.

Waking and sleeping are two states of existence. Without the desire and the practice, recollections from one state of existence are not carried into the other. Many people know that they dream, but they cannot remember what their dreams were. Remembering dreams, and making sense out of them, is but a matter of training and practice. I'm convinced that this chapter will give you the help you need to use your sleep to learn about your future.

Mrs. A. B. of San Francisco recently told me of a dream she had during World War II.

My husband was stationed on an island in the Pacific. His normal duties had nothing to do with airplanes and I couldn't understand a dream that I had. It was so detailed. It concerned a plane falling—and him in it! As he had been out about

twenty-three months, we both hoped he would
soon be relieved to return home. I wrote him the
very next morning after the dream asking him not
to think of flying home. If he was relieved, he
should come by ship even though it took longer.
He wrote to me the same day (we numbered and
dated each letter). Our letters crossed in midair.
The letter I received told me of his very dangerous
mission to fly to check the camouflage of the island. He was quite upset about the dives and other
maneuvers of the airplane. The man who took a
similar run the next day was killed.

Mrs. B. (who, by the way, was an excellent psychic) had been receiving psychic impulses that her
husband was in danger. But because of her emotional
attachment she could not clear her mind to accept
them consciously. When she went to sleep, her mental
anxiety was relieved, and her spirit was free to accept
messages unencumbered.

Types of Dreams

There are three major types of dreams: the physical,
the allegorical, and the literal.

The *physical* dream has no psychic meaning or
origin. Physical dreams result from your mind continuing to dominate the spirit even though you are
asleep. If you sleep on a lumpy mattress or are too cold
or too warm, you have nonsensical dreams that are
fantasies of your imagination. These fantasies may also
occur when you're overtired or emotionally upset. You
may also experience nightmares. Dreams are not the
exception to the psychic rule that a peaceful mind and
a relaxed body are essential to valid psychic communication.

Allegorical dreams are mental experiences that

have an obvious truth in their center, but the circumstances surrounding the theme of the dream are unreal. An example of an allegorical dream has been shared by a conscientious church-goer:

> On a Sunday night I awoke with a start. I dreamt that my pastor and his co-pastor had beaten me. I asked myself (in the dream), why? I wasn't anyplace I shouldn't have been. What did I do? The next flash, the pastor was sitting down in a chair. With the left side of my face bruised, I asked him, "Why did you do it?" He was upset and answered, "I wasn't there to prevent it."
>
> I sensed immediately that I either had or was going to do something that needed a reprimand. I was going to tread softly. I mentioned my dream to a co-member of our board of trustees. We wondered what our coming monthly board meeting would hold.
>
> Tuesday evening the board of trustees was reprimanded for their lack of spiritual understanding. At the previous month's meeting we had all been asked to do a simple spiritual exercise that would have taken about an hour of our time. Each one of us had thought, "The others will do it!" As a result, not one person had fulfilled the request. My *spiritual* beating!

This is an interesting example of an allegorical dream. The theme of the dream was true—a reprimand or spiritual beating. The circumstances surrounding the reprimand were entirely unreal: the pastor and co-pastor were committed to nonviolence. It is an allegorical dream if a very logical occurrence is surrounded by very illogical circumstances.

One night I dreamt of a man I knew. I respected

this man because of the high position he held. In the dream the man had died. His casket was sitting in the middle of an amphitheater, and I was the only one there. As I looked at the casket, I saw hundreds of snakes crawling from it.

It wasn't too long after this dream that the man did die. I attended the funeral. With the exception of family members, I was the only other person at the funeral.

Hundreds of people had flocked around this gentleman in life. But it was his position and not he that was admired. This was reflected in their absence from his funeral.

An English friend told me of a recurrent allegorical dream that she had many years ago. She lived in London, while the remainder of her family lived in a small town hundreds of miles away.

For several nights in a row, this lady had a dream of the walls falling down at her family home. Then one night she dreamed that the entire house had collapsed. The dream disturbed her so much that she placed an immediate telephone call to her parents' home. Her sister answered the telephone. "I'm so glad you called. Daddy just died!" For that family, the walls did come tumbling down.

You *Are* Susceptible to the Thoughts of Others

You may not believe that you are susceptible to the thoughts of others, but you are. Thoughts are real things. But it is during your sleep that thoughts from others have the greatest opportunity to influence you—for good or ill. Let me tell you about an experiment that one of my classes performed.

Without explaining the reason, I asked one of the class members to leave the room. After she had gone, I asked the remaining class members to concentrate on making the lady out of the room dream that very night that there was a great deal of confusion and irritation within the class.

After a few minutes of concentration, the lady was asked to come back into the room. The class continued in its normal sequence until we were ready to conclude for the evening. It was at that time that I "asked" the class to participate in an additional project—one they had already been told was meant to fool our subject. I asked them to write down any dreams that they might have that particular night. (Only the woman who left the room thought the assignment was real.)

At the next class meeting I asked the lady who had left the room the previous week to begin the class by telling us if she had had any dreams on the previous class night. "Yes, I did," she answered. This is what the woman had written concerning her dream.

> I was at a dinner and there was a feeling of uneasiness—everyone from the class was there. Bob [the author] made a ceremony of using tiny squares of cloth to wash each finger separately. I found it very irritating that he was showing us how to do it properly, and even more irritating that all of the class was doing the same thing. In many ways Bob seemed to be serious, and in other ways it seemed to be a big joke.

Obviously, the feelings of confusion and irritation the class concentrated on did manifest themselves in the lady's dream.

For practical purposes, everyone should try to make themselves immune to the negative thoughts of others. This can be done easily by simple affirmation. At bedtime say something like, "I am not susceptible to the thoughts of others during my sleep." A simple affirmation is sufficient to ward off any unwelcome mental imbalance.

The *literal* dream is sometimes difficult to differentiate from a dream fantasy. The literal dream is so realistic that you may question whether you had a dream or not.

As real as a literal dream may seem, however, there will always be something within the dream that is obviously out of place. An exaggerated example might be a dream that takes place within a room that is completely white except for one black spot on the carpeting. Or you might dream of a scene that is very familiar to you, but notice that one object normally there is missing. When you note in your dream that something is out of place, you can be 100 percent sure that your dream has been literal, or prophetic, in nature.

A close friend had a recurrent dream that was, at least to me, obviously literal or prophetic. He swore that the dream could not be prophetic because he would "never do what the dream was showing" him doing.

In my friend's dream he was standing behind a church pulpit looking out over the congregation. Each time that he had this dream, he noticed that there were flowers on the altar in inappropriate containers.

In a few years, my friend was the pastor of one of the fastest growing churches of its denomination in the country.

Experience will prove that it is unlikely that the prophecy contained within the literal dream will, or can, change. You might delay the manifestation of the prophecy by making its manifestation difficult to achieve, but the dream will come true.

How Dreams Help Maintain Good Mental Health

Dreams are an interesting phenomenon—from both a psychic and a psychological point of view. I personally believe that it is dreams that help keep us sane and sensible people. Many psychologists agree. Dreams, much more often than is reported in the textbooks, are used by many people to drag themselves from what seem to be psychological disasters.

A married couple I became acquainted with did maintain their happiness and stability through dreams, when everything else was lost to them, even psychological counseling.

The couple had a very prosperous business that suddenly went bankrupt because of the introduction of a more efficient product by a competitor. They were forced to sell their home, their summer cabin, and even their automobile to satisfy their creditors. Their jet-set social life and foreign vacations became a thing of the past.

When they found it impossible to live within their new spartan means they contemplated suicide. When their emotional low had been hit—when they believed that they could no longer bear one more day of their new existence—they began having dreams of fantasy (or hope). Their dreams were of the foreign countries they had visited in the past. Their previous social life. And they dreamed of owning more material possessions than they had at even their most affluent. Many times they shared identical dreams (a phenomenon against which the odds are astronomical).

I talked with these people about their dreams. I asked if they didn't feel it psychologically unhealthy to live in a world of fantasy. Their reply was an emphatic no.

The dreams were very real to them. They were as

enjoyable as the experiences had been in reality. Their happy dreams at night were making their unhappy days more bearable. And they never lost sight of the fact that their fantasies were dreams—to be used as a temporary and not as a permanent crutch to their emotional ills.

Several months later I again saw the same couple. They told me they had gained back a portion of their material wealth and were quite content with what material security they now had. Their most revealing comment was, "Our fantasies decreased in direct proportion to the material success we gained. Dreams are the best psychiatrist in the world."

Dreams were the best psychiatrist for that couple, but dreams are not necessarily the best psychological answer to every problem—it depends upon each individual. I in no way imply that psychologists and psychiatrists be ignored after you've completed this chapter. Those professionals have their place, and their knowledge should be used. And, if you have need of such professional advice, you just may be happily surprised that your psychologist will approve your dream therapy—documenting it all the way to its successful conclusion.

THE UNHEALTHY FANTASY

Joanne was deeply infatuated with the young man next door, whom we'll call Paul. Paul was not the least interested in Joanne. In fact, he went out of his way to be rude.

Joanne began having dreams about Paul. In her dreams, Paul showered her with affection. He told her that he was wild about her, but shy—he didn't want to express his true feelings in front of others.

Joanne told her mother, father, and her friends of the "true feelings" that Paul felt toward her. "He's crazy about me and wants me to become his wife," she said. When Paul married another woman, Joanne had a very serious mental breakdown.

This dream of fantasy was obviously unhealthy, and, more important, it was not a literal or prophetic dream. But how can you tell the difference?

Joanne had been a spoiled child. She received her every desire, either through pleading or a tantrum—whichever was the quickest way to the fulfillment of her desires. Since as an adult, Joanne couldn't kick or scream, she threw herself into the fantasy of the dream. Her sleep was not deep and peaceful. It was constant tossing and turning, waking up perspiring several times during the night. Joanne's dreams were physical and psychological. They were not literal or prophetic. A spoiled brat had an overactive imagination. Her dreams were nothing more.

Prophetic Dreaming

If you have an interest in prophetic dreaming it must become a habit—second nature, if you want it to be a satisfying, successful experience.

To experience prophetic dreaming you must, just before dozing off, tell your conscious mind that you are going to remember your dream upon awakening in the morning. If you have a specific thing you want to dream about, think of it. If not, dream at random.

If you awaken during the night, jot down your dreams on a pad of paper that should be kept on your nightstand. Do the same thing in the morning: jot down all of your dream memories before the cares of the day make you forget the dreams.

Very recently a gentleman who had attended my billet demonstrations for almost a year approached me after a meeting. He told me that all of his billets had concerned jobs, and that his questions had always been answered. He'd be told when he'd get a new job and he would—but he'd soon lose that job. He'd come back for another billet reading, receive an answer, get the job, and lose it again. "Why can't I keep a job?" he asked.

I suggested that rather than ask me that question, he ask himself for the answer through dreaming. I explained how to do it.

A month later he talked to me again. "That dream bit doesn't work," he told me in sarcastic tones. "I dreamed the same damned thing every night and it didn't make any sense at all."

"What did you dream?" I asked.

"I dreamt that I was hiding in a trench from soldiers who kept walking by looking for me."

The man had experienced an allegorical dream.

I told the fellow that he had received the answer to his question but hadn't bothered to accept it.

I asked him, "What do soldiers mean to you?"

His answer was: "Conflict."

I then asked him what a trench symbolized to him.

"A trench means insecurity to me," he snapped out. I pointed out the obvious answer to his question.

His conflict, his inability to hold a job, was due to his own feeling of insecurity. That's why he was hiding in the trench from the soldiers.

The man still was not satisfied. "I didn't need a dream to tell me that I had an inferiority complex. What I needed to dream was how to get over the insecurity. This dreaming stuff is a bunch of baloney."

But was it baloney? No!

How to get over his insecurity was not the question he had asked. The question asked was, "Why am I unable to keep a job?" That question *was* answered.

DREAMS CANNOT MAKE FANTASIES A REALITY

Common sense! Common sense! Common sense! Repeat the words until you're tired of hearing them.

Common sense buttresses you against the temptation to become a "psychic weirdo." Let me give an example.

A very good friend of mine decided that she wanted to get into astrophysics. Night after night she failed in her attempts to dream any prophecies concerning her future desires. She was totally dismayed. But let me explain something.

My friend, bless her, can't even balance her checkbook. How could she possibly become a physicist? She couldn't. If you ask for a prophetic dream concerning such an "off-the-wall" question as the one asked by my friend, you'll get the same answer: nothing.

Accepting Your Own Psychic Impressions

I've been involved in the psychic world a good many years, and there are still times when I rebel against accepting my psychic impressions. I should, and I do, know better. But there are instances when even I just can't accept what I psychically receive. I'm not sure why this happens at one time and not another, but it does. Undoubtedly it will happen to you as well. Don't be alarmed. It's a temporary aberration.

Every talented person suffers sporadic feelings of insecurity. Your talent may be of a psychic nature, but it does, very often, give you what is usually termed "the artistic temperament."

A former student wrote me:

> I was very dissatisfied with my job. I would receive psychic impressions on how to correct the situation. I would think about it and then decide that my ESP didn't make any sense. After a while, I started having what I knew to be prophetic dreams. These dreams showed me, step by step,

what the results would be if I followed my psychic impressions. I accepted the dreams, but I do remember thinking, "Boy, will things really have to change before that dream can come true."

I followed my psychic impressions. My dissatisfaction was removed and I was placed in a wonderfully satisfying work environment. The new job was by no means strange or unfamiliar when I made the change. I had dreamed of it so strongly and clearly that I even knew exactly what each person in my new department was going to say before I was introduced to them.

Whenever you have difficulty looking at a personal situation in an objective manner, confirm your intuition by dreaming. Your sub-conscious distancing from the problem during sleep allows a greater freedom for the spirit to dominate the mind and to produce an accurate reply to your question.

You are not going to receive an immediate answer to every dream question that you ask. Dreaming is no different from developing any other psychic talent. You have to practice. If you don't receive an answer to your question on the first night, ask the same question again the next night. Oftentimes, our questions require such complex answers that our minds are not capable of understanding the answer on its first pass into our consciousness.

Interpreting Your Allegorical Dreams

You've just awakened from an allegorical dream and you write it down quickly—right? That's the only way to derive an accurate interpretation of your dream. You now follow much the same procedure that you followed in the chapters on symbols and the aura. I might write a dream down in this manner:

> I was standing by a dirt road watching people walk by. They walked very slowly with their heads down so that I couldn't see their faces. In the distance I could see a red bridge over a river. On the other side of the river I saw a pagoda. The sky was very dark as if a furious storm was about to begin.

I would list the symbols from my allegorical dream like this:

1. A dirt road
    Countryside
2. People walking with heads down
    Sadness or mourning
3. A red bridge
    Passing from this world to the next
4. River
    River
5. Pagoda
    Chinese
6. Dark storm clouds
    Heavy rain or flooding

After breaking my dream down in this manner, the allegorical dream appears as this: Many people will soon be killed in China because of heavy flooding. This allegorical dream example was a prediction I gave at a New Year's Eve party. Unfortunately, it did come true shortly after the prediction.

A good editor is a treasure to cling to. My own editor asked me a question concerning the interpretation of this particular dream that I hadn't even thought to explain. He asked, "How did you interpret the symbols in your allegorical dream? How did you know 'pagoda' meant China, but that 'river' meant only a river?"

The most direct way to address this very logical question is to make the explanation simple, which it actually is.

I know my symbols well, as you now do or soon will. A pagoda always represents China to me whenever, or however, I see it in my psychic vision.

Unless there is an unnatural element in my vision of a river—its waters are golden in color, or whatever— an ordinary-looking river is simply that, a river.

Recalling Dreams at a Later Time

How often have you been in a social or other gathering, to discover that everything about it is familiar? You've even heard identical conversations before that party. Sometimes people think of this as a "déjà vu" or "having been there before" experience, but often it is, instead, the result of a precognitive dream. That is, the scene seems familiar not because you have *lived* it before, but because you have *foreseen* it in a dream.

The notion of déjà vu leads to the subject of reincarnation, which is beyond the scope of this book. Let me say for now simply that encountering a situation that you have previously dreamed is more common than you might think.

It is not an exceptional person who remembers dreams at a later time. It is the exceptional person who does *not* remember dreams at a later time.

What About Doctors?

Doctors are a very important fact of life. Psychic healing and medicine should work in unison. The real secret of healing is not to become ill in the first place, but once ill, by all means see a physician as well as a psychic healer.

I am in constant contact with psychic healers. They do a good job in keeping people from becoming ill so that a doctor's visit isn't needed in the first place. The healer's thoughts and actions do much to increase the personal awareness within the individual. This awareness leads the person to investigate his mode of living, and where necessary to correct its deficiencies—in effect causing good health.

Is "Faith" Necessary for Healing?

No! Faith is not necessary for healing. It helps because faith requires confidence and positive thinking. Where there is positive thinking there is a striving for peace and harmony. When people strive for peace and harmony they strive to remove the cause of an illness (either consciously or subconsciously).

There are literally thousands of recorded case histories affirming that when a healer was asked to heal an individual without that person's knowledge, healing that could not be attributed to any other factor did occur.

There are a number of psychic healers who work exclusively with animals. The animal does not have faith and yet can be healed.

The Universal Healing Law

If you accept the premise that the entire universe is governed by law, you can more readily understand how a nonbeliever can be healed as well as a believer. *A universal law will work in its own particular fashion whether it is believed in or not.*

An analogy might be a person who has never seen an electric light. You could ask the person if he believed that the glass bulb could shed light. He would deny that a globe of glass could produce light. You ask him to flick the light switch, and the bulb produces light. The light is the result of a natural law. The belief or disbelief of the person who flicked the switch did not change the manifestation of that law. Disbelief in the healing law does not change its effect any more than the disbelief in the ability of a glass globe to produce light changes its effect.

Are Some Things More Difficult to Heal Than Others?

Statistically, any illness that is manmade, such as an excess of certain chemicals, cigarettes, and alcoholism, is more difficult to heal than other illnesses.

Psychic healing works slowly in areas of the body where the structure has been changed through operations.

Affirmities and ailments that are due to old age are less likely to respond to psychic healing than are other diseases. Nature demands that we grow old. The healer cannot change a natural law of the universe.

Young children most usually respond favorably to psychic healing. Beyond the physical strength and vitality of youth, the child is less likely to be encumbered by mental negativity.

Case Histories

Here are two letters that were given to me concerning psychic healing. Perhaps the testimonials will shed a revealing light on some of your questions about psychic healing.

> I seldom feel the need to sit for a healing, but there have been things that have bothered me, and psychic healing has given me the help that I needed in a very short time.
>
> A severe pain in my foot caused me to limp and feel pain with each step. After a healing, I walked without pain.
>
> Recently I was eating sweets just prior to a healing service and I got a severe toothache. While I received a psychic healing, my husband was looking for the telephone number of an emergency dentist. He needn't have bothered. The pain left with the healing.
>
> D.K.
> San Francisco

The next testimonial is from a young woman who discovered that she had a tumor on her thyroid gland. (The difference between this testimonial and the prior one is the partnership between the physician and the healer. That the psychic healer happened to be the girl's mother shouldn't have a bearing on this case, but it does! The girl who wrote the testimonial was a loving and trusting young woman. The trust she felt toward her mother she also shared with her physician.)

> The first doctor I went to for an examination was standing against a white wall explaining the details of my tumor. Suddenly I saw a large light-blue figure looming up on the right side of the doctor. As light blue means "very spiritual" to me, I thought, "I must be in the right place."
>
> Another incident occurred while taking tests

in the hospital. I was placed under the radioactive isotope scanner. As I was lying in the semi-darkened room looking at the dark trap door in the ceiling, I noticed that the door turned white in color—white being the highest spiritual color. Just then a long ear-piercing scream came from the machine. Technicians were sent scurrying to turn it off. The doctor was called in and found that the X-ray picture was working fine, but that the other part of the test just went wild and would not work.

My doctor then sent me to a vascular surgeon. As the surgeon was drawing diagrams to show me how he was going to operate, I looked up and saw two misty-white forms. One on each side of him—as if angels were watching every detail.

My mother had received some brief training in psychic healing but had never practiced it. When she placed her hands on my throat they began to shake violently. Her hands were stuck to my neck and she couldn't remove them. When her hands were finally released, my collar was soaked with a fluid that came through my skin. The tumor felt smaller and softer. I saw my doctor the next day. He confirmed that the tumor was softer and smaller, but he couldn't explain why.

The most reassuring thing of all was the great healing force that I saw swirling around the hospital room on the night before surgery.

After the surgery, the doctor told me that he was positive that a facial nerve on the left side of my face had been bruised and that I should expect a permanent twitch. I did not develop a twitch!

Another amazing thing was that the docotrs and nurses were surprised that I felt no pain or discomfort of any kind following the surgery. Instead, I was full of vitality and very hungry. In fact,

after I had finished off the liquid breakfast served
to me, I ordered eggs, bacon and toast.

B.C.
San Jose

I believe there is more doubt about the effec-
tiveness of psychic healing than of any other ESP
talent. For this I'm personally thankful. Too many
people are inclined to discard medical doctors for psychic healers before they think their decision through.
Why not both?

I could fill a book with testimonials and examples
of successful psychic healing, but that is not my purpose. For those who wish documentation and testimonials by both patients and physicians, I suggest you
visit your public library and seek out books written by
or about Harry Edwards, a famous English healer who
passed away quite recently. All of the books were pub-
lished in England, but are available in the United
States. To my knowledge, Mr. Edwards was the most
thoroughly scientifically investigated psychic healer of
modern times.

If you doubt the possibility of healing, keep at
least an open mind until you discover for yourself if it's
fact or fancy. Your conclusion should be the result of
your own judgment and observation. That is what *ESP
for Everyone* is all about.

Psychic Healing and Your Own Health

You don't need a psychic development book to remind
you that balanced diet, adequate sleep, and mental
relaxation are the builders of good health. Keep up
those good habits and use your psychic ability to see if
there is an illness in your future because you're ne-

glecting other good health habits. Then change your habits to prevent the illness. Don't knowingly practice bad health habits thinking that when you're flat on your back, you can use psychic healing to restore your health.

We live in a rush-rush society. Unfortunately there are times that life does require us to burn the candle at both ends, but you need not become ill over the extra burden placed on your mental and physical resources. Listen to your instinct. When that "inner voice" says that your limit has been reached, stop! If you don't stop, be willing to accept the consequences.

Each of you is most probably acquainted with a hypochondriac. They are ill because they believe that they are ill. Conversely, healthy people are that way because they believe they are.

The most positive health advice that I can share with you is this: *Believe that you are healthy and you will be healthy.* If something occurs in your life that might destroy your perfect health, your intuition will reveal how you can counter this negative influence before it manifests itself in your body as an illness. If you pay attention to the voice of your subconscious mind you will always be warned *before* an illness strikes.

11

The Magic Wand You Make for Yourself

Your basic commonsense psychic development lessons are now complete. I'd like to have a magic wand—a magic wand to touch each of you with and declare, "You are a clairvoyant, you are a clairaudient, you possess clairsentience." But that would only be a gimmick. You already have those powers.

If there is a magic wand, it's a wand that you create for yourself. You build it by hard work, patience, practice, and honorable motives.

In this book I have ignored what is commonly termed astral projection. It is undoubtedly an interesting subject, and it can be a thrilling phenomenon when personally experienced. But too many moral, ethical, and psychological questions remain in my own mind concerning the subject to allow me to teach it with complete conviction and vigor.

You may have unanswered questions that arose during the psychic lessons. I hope that you have questions, but it is literally impossible in a book of this nature to answer each and every question that might arise. This does not mean that your questions will remain unanswered. The answers will reveal themselves as you practice and develop the psychic skills that you already possess. Just don't worry about it. At this point, you know what you need to know.

How to Use Your Psychic Potential to Build a More Abundant Life

Your newly discovered psychic abilities may prove to be entertaining for demonstration purposes. There's no question that the psychic world is a great subject of conversation when talk begins to drag, but remember that your instinct and your intuition have a more practical value than this. The practical value is the manner in which you use instinct to build a more abundant, peaceful, healthy, and happy life.

How to Realize the Potential of Your Newfound Psychic Power

Walk before you run! You must be totally convinced that you possess a tool that can, and will, enrich your life. You must build your abilities step by step until you reach the zenith of your psychic goals. Begin by using your psychic abilities in the smaller, less important areas of your life. When these results authenticate your psychic impressions, take a step forward into attaining larger goals.

How to Build a Positive Attitude Toward Wealth

Wealth means many things to many people. To one person it means having more money than can possibly be spent. To another wealth means simply having a roof over the head and enough to eat. People have used my lessons to achieve successfully both degrees of wealth. They consciously went after what wealth they desired, and they achieved it. I believe, however, that both extremes are transitory in nature. The emphasis in my classes has been the "middle-road" approach.

The accumulation of more wealth than one needs can imply fear of the future—money as a security blanket in case things happen to go wrong. Accumulation of excess wealth can also arise from simple selfishness. Neither of these are positive. Certainly, it's great to have money. I wish I had more. Just don't fear poverty, or you will draw it to you. Respect money, but don't desire money for the sake of money alone.

The other side of the coin is to absolutely trust that when you have need of money, you'll have it. The simple satisfaction of food on the table and a roof over your head can signal a negative approach to wealth if you believe that's all you can have, that it's impossible to increase your wealth. If you live that simple life because it brings joy and happiness, and you know that you can achieve more if you have the desire, then you're living as prosperous a life as any individual can.

You should simply be aware that ESP can help you achieve more prosperity. But also remember that you have to do something before you receive it. It just doesn't fall out of the sky.

REALIZE HOW IMPORTANT YOU REALLY ARE

If you do not believe that you are a very important person, you can feel assured that no one else will believe it either. Regardless of your past thinking, you must now realize what an important person you really are. Nothing would, or could, happen in your world without *you.*

There are many successful people who erroneously believe that it is not spiritual, and is egotistical, to believe in the importance of one's self. But if you have no self-esteem, your life is tossed to and fro by the whims and fancies of others. It is only when you accept the universal fact that you are an important person that you are able to resist domination by those whose interests run contrary to your own. It would be unwise to believe that you are the most important person in the world, but it would be equally unwise to believe that you are less important than any other person.

A famous psychiatrist, a very caring human being who ran one of the largest groups of mental health facilities in the nation, told me, "It's so very sad. The hardest person for an individual to learn to like is himself."

Let me ask a question to which no one will know the answer but yourself: "Do you like yourself?"

The majority of honest answers will either be "no" or "I'm not sure." If your answer is either of the above, success is difficult under any circumstances. Psychic ability rarely achieves permanent positive results for the person who has not learned to like himself or herself. Temporary success can be achieved by the psychic person who feels that way, but the results are short-lived. In that case, the failures and unhappiness encountered by a person who doesn't like himself are inevitably blamed on the involvement with psychic phenomena.

Your path to success is clear. Simply change your attitude. Forgive your errors and praise the good that you do. Throw the thought away that you're going to be a "perfect" person; you won't be. But you can be a very, very good person who recognizes the same good in every other person.

I must emphasize this one fact. Liking or not liking yourself does not in any manner reflect upon the accuracy of any psychic information that you give to anyone through billet reading, independent reading, aura analysis, and the like. The conflict only touches the psychic information that is received for yourself, not others.

How to Transfer Your Psychic Energy to Where It Is Needed

If you have an immediate problem, whether it is mental or physical fatigue, misunderstandings with other individuals, unfair treatment, lack of money, or an illness, you should transfer all of your psychic energy to the source of the problem. This is not as difficult as it may seem.

Concentrated psychic energy is a force of power that can and should be used at every opportunity. And it works!

First you must honestly identify the problem. You must then remove the emotional negativity you feel toward the problem. The third step is sometimes less easy because of your inevitable emotional condition, but you must conjure up a feeling of power within yourself so that you feel an almost tingling sensation. When this level of consciousness is reached, mentally "hurl" the energy to the source of your problem. As you do, voice a positive affirmation: "Right action now corrects and solves my problem. Harmony now prevails in my world."

HOW TO BUILD A MAGNETIC PERSONALITY

Successful people share many characteristics, but there is none more noticeable than the "magnetic" personality. People are not born with this magnetism, they develop it. And so must you. Here's how:

1. Approach all tasks with confidence.
2. No matter how unimportant a task may appear, do it well.
3. Know that you are an important person.
4. Like yourself!
5. *Follow the guidance of your instinct and intuition—even if it appears contrary to the facts at hand.* (This step performs miracles only if you are successful in the first four steps.)

HOW TO STRENGTHEN THE POWER OF YOUR SUBCONSCIOUS MIND

Your physical muscles grow and strengthen through exercise. The same is true with the subconscious mind. If you want to strengthen it, use it! Use it as you learned in the lessons contained in this book and use it by constantly affirming that "the impulses of my subconscious mind are accepted and manifested within my conscious mind."

CONDITION YOUR MIND TO ACCEPT YOUR NEW WAY OF LIFE

You're reading this book because it contains subject matter that you hope can enrich your life in one way or another—and it's a hope I believe will be fulfilled. But many of you are already successful in most areas of your life. It's to those who are not successful that I particularly address the next two paragraphs.

Old habits are hard to break. If, at the present time, you are less successful than you want to be, you must condition your mind to accept new and changing circumstances. You must accept and adapt to change.

People sometimes say, "I want this and I want that," and then paradoxically say, "but I don't want to change." It *can't* be both ways. Any new way of life, whether due to success or failure, requires change and adjustment. *Be prepared to make and accept changes.*

LEARN FROM THOSE WHO HAVE ALREADY ACHIEVED SUCCESS

ESP for Everyone will help you to achieve success. It will not *make* you a success. Intellectual common sense and psychic common sense are siamese twins. One should not attempt to separate them. They share a common heartbeat. Don't kill one to save the other. Let your intellectual common sense direct you to the observation and study of those who have already achieved success; your psychic common sense will direct you to the best method(s) to use in achieving these goals.

APPENDIX

Psychic Phenomena and the Bible

> But the manifestation of the Spirit is given to every man to profit withal. For to one is given by the Spirit the word of wisdom; to another the word of knowledge by the same Spirit; to another faith by the same Spirit; to another the gift of healing by the same Spirit; to another the working of miracles; to another prophecy; to another discerning of spirits; to another divers kinds of tongues; to another the interpretation of tongues.
>
> —I Corinthians 12:7–10

Dreams As Psychic Phenomena

The most memorable examples of dreams as psychic phenomena can be found in the experiences of Joseph, the father of Jesus. Of the five dreams of Joseph, I can safely say that without their occurrence there would be no Christianity.

Joseph's first dream concerned the birth and divinity of Jesus (Matthew 1:20). His second dream warned of the danger to the little boy (Matthew 2:12). The third dream sent Joseph, Mary, and Jesus to Egypt (Matthew 2:13). The fourth dream was of the death of Herod (Matthew 2:19). The fifth dream sent the family of Jesus back to Nazareth (Matthew 2:22).

Dreams are an integral part of psychic phenomena, and this psychic talent continues to be as active today as it was 2,000 years ago (and ages before) in the Old Testament.

In the twenty-eighth chapter of Genesis can be read the familiar story of Jacob's ladder: "And he dreamed, and behold a ladder set up on the earth, and the top of it reached heaven. . . ."

In Genesis 31:24 we read: "And God came to Laban the Syrian in a dream by night, and said unto him, Take heed that thou speak not Jacob either good or bad."

In Genesis 37:5 there's a wonderful story of Joseph: "And Joseph dreamed a dream, and he told it to his brethren . . ." and another in Genesis 44:1: "And it came to pass at the end of two full years, that Pharaoh dreamed . . ."

Clairaudience (Clear Hearing)

"And he fell to the earth, and heard a voice saying unto him, Saul, Saul, why persecutest thou me?" This is a dramatic story of clairaudience. Here is Saul walking toward Damascus in hope of finding disciples of Jesus so that they might be persecuted. A voice is heard (clairaudiently, we must assume, as there is no record that Saul's companions heard the voice), and the history of the world was changed.

The Old Testament, Job 4:12–16, gives an instance of both clairaudience and clairvoyance.

> Now a thing was secretly brought to me and mine ear received a little thereof, in thoughts from the visions of the night, when deep sleep falleth on men, fear came upon me, and trembling, which made all my bones to shake. Then a spirit passed

before my face; the hair of my flesh stood up; It
stood still, but I could not discern the form thereof;
an image was before mine eyes, there was silence,
and I heard a voice.

These are only two of dozens of scriptural references
to clairaudience.

Clairvoyance (Clear Seeing)

With the possible exception of healing, there are more
references to clairvoyance in the Bible than other intuitive or psychic powers.

An interesting reference to clairvoyance occurs on
the Mount of Transfiguration. Jesus took Peter, James,
and John "into a high mountain apart . . . and there
appeared unto them Moses and Elias talking with
him." Later in the chapter Jesus says, "Tell the vision
to no man." Obviously a psychic experience had occurred. The example refers to clairvoyance, for Jesus
uses the word *vision*, which is synonymous with *clairvoyance*.

In II Kings 6:17, Elisha prays that the gift of
"sight" be granted to his servant. We read: ". . . I pray
thee, open his eyes, that he may see. And the Lord
opened the eyes of the young man; and he saw: and
behold, the mountain was full of horses and chariots of
fire around about Elisha." He could not have referred
to a physical blindness of the servant. In that day, it
was very unlikely that anyone would have a blind servant.

Telepathy

How often have you been thinking of someone when
suddenly the telephone rings and it's the person you

were thinking of? Telepathy, thought transference, ESP, or whatever you'd like to call it is such a common occurrence that I believe even the most skeptical of persons would have to admit "there's *something* there" that cannot be explained by conventional reasoning.

Just two of the many references to telepathy are in Matthew 9:4 and Luke 5:22. We read in the former that Jesus, having passed over in the ship to his own city, was confronted by the scribes who thought he had committed blasphemy by healing on the Sabbath "and Jesus knowing their thoughts said, wherefore think ye evil in your hearts?" In the latter it is then written: "But when Jesus perceived their thoughts, he answering said unto them, what reason ye in your hearts?"

Prophecy

Prophecy is the psychic talent that enables one to foresee or foretell events that will occur in the future.

> And it shall come to pass in the last days, saith God, I will pour out of my Spirit upon all flesh: and your sons and your daughters shall prophesy, and your young men shall see visions, and your old men shall dream dreams; And on my servants and on my handmaidens I will pour out in those days of my Spirit; and they shall prophesy.

> Acts 2:17–18

In Acts 19:6 we read of prophecy in the same manner as being an "independent message," of the same sort as you learned about earlier in this book: "And when Paul had laid his hands upon them, the Holy Ghost came on them; and they spake with tongues, and prophesied." In verse 21 of Acts 27, we read: "But after long abstinence Paul stood forth in the midst of them, and said, Sirs, ye should hearken unto me, and not have loosed from Crete, and to have joined this harm and loss." In verses 26, 31, and 34, is the remainder of the prophecy: "Howbeit we must be cast upon a certain island? . . . Paul said to the centurion and to the soldiers, Except these abide in the ship, ye cannot be saved. . . . Wherefore I pray you to take some meat; for this is for your health; for there shall not an hair fall from the head of any of you."

In the twelfth chapter of I Corinthians, verses 4 through 11, we read the beautiful words concerning prophecy and other "gifts" of the spirit:

Now there are diversities of gifts, but the same Spirit. And there are differences of administrations, but the same Lord. And there are diversities of operations, but it is the same God which worketh all in all. But the manifestation of the Spirit is given to every man to profit withal. For to one is given by the Spirit the word of wisdom; to another, the word of knowledge by the same Spirit; to another, faith by the same Spirit; to another, the gift of healing by the same Spirit; to another, the working of miracles; to another, prophecy; to another, discerning of spirits; to another, divers kinds of tongues; to another, the interpretation of tongues; But all these worketh that one and the selfsame Spirit, dividing to every man severally as he will.

HERE'S HOW

HOW TO BUY A CAR by James R. Ross
The essential guide that gives you the edge in buying a new or used car.
_____ 90198-4 $3.95 U.S.   _____ 90199-2 $4.95 Can.

THE WHOLESALE-BY-MAIL CATALOG—UPDATE 1986 by The Print Project
Everything you need at 30% to 90% off retail prices—by mail or phone!
_____ 90379-0 $3.95 U.S.   _____ 90380-4 $4.95 Can.

TAKING CARE OF CLOTHES: An Owner's Manual for Care, Repair and Spot Removal by Mablen Jones
The most comprehensive handbook of its kind...save money—and save your wardrobe!
_____ 90355-3 $4.95 U.S.   _____ 90356-1 $5.95 Can.

AND THE LUCKY WINNER IS...The Complete Guide to Winning Sweepstakes & Contests
by Carolyn and Roger Tyndall with Tad Tyndall
Increase the odds in your favor—all you need to know.
_____ 90025-2 $3.95 U.S.   _____ 90026-0 $4.95 Can.

THE OFFICIAL HARVARD STUDENT AGENCIES BARTENDING COURSE
The new complete guide to drinkmaking—the $40 course now a paperback book!
_____ 90427-4 $3.95 U.S.   _____ 90430-4 $4.95 Can.

Publishers Book and Audio Mailing Service
P.O. Box 120159, Staten Island, NY 10312-0004

Please send me the book(s) I have checked above. I am enclosing
$ _____ (please add $1.25 for the first book, and $.25 for each additional book to cover postage and handling. Send check or money order only—no CODs.)

Name _____

Address _____

City _____ State/Zip _____

Please allow six weeks for delivery. Prices subject to change without notice.

HOW 1/89

NONFICTION PERENNIALS
FROM ST. MARTIN'S PRESS

Eternal Wisdom for Today's Lifestyles

LINDA GOODMAN'S STAR SIGNS

Linda Goodman is the most respected name in astrology and metaphysics. With her usual compassion, wit, and perception, she has now written the definitive guide to putting established knowledge to work for all her readers in today's fast-paced world. It will lead you to discover your latent powers, to control your personal destiny, and to recall the forgotten harmony of the Universe.

LINDA GOODMAN'S STAR SIGNS

_____ 91263-3 $4.95 U.S.   _____ 91264-1 $5.95 Can.

10

Psychic Energy and the Power of Healing

Psychic healing, or spiritual healing, as many refer to it, remains a controversial subject within and without the world of ESP. I suggest that much of the controversy could be avoided if publicity seekers who ply healing as a trade and those university researchers who submit questionable statistics in order to continue receiving grants just keep quiet for a while until the dust settles.

Persons who hold extreme positions either for or against psychic healing accomplish little of a positive nature. A closed mind is hardly susceptible to new ideas or new research. If you have an interest in psychic or spiritual healing, travel the middle road. Keep an open mind, use common sense, and then draw your own conclusions while ignoring when others tell you what you should or should not believe.

183

Inconsistencies Remain

I would like to pass on to you, the reader, my own opinion, based on what I've observed over the years, concerning psychic healing.

First, I'm not completely comfortable with psychic healing, and I've had limited success in performing it. Rather than heal a person, *I* would pick up all of the symptoms too, which did neither one of us any good.

I have watched as people with major illnesses were completely healed. I have also observed that there are people with minor complaints that are not healed. Why? It's a question waiting for an answer.

I have been convinced that psychic healing can work, but it has taken many years of observation, and I still don't believe it **always** works. I had always believed that psychic healing was *possible* and I kept an open mind on the subject. I just did not meet any psychics who were in fact accomplishing any psychic healings—regardless of their many boasts of the cures that had come through their "healing hands." Later association did put me in contact with psychic healers who were in fact accomplishing healings that could not be attributed to other sources.

In this chapter I'll attempt to steer you on the right road toward psychic healing, but it's *your* responsibility to develop your own healing philosophy and reach your own conclusions.

The Philosophy of Healing and the Nature of Illness

There are as many philosophies of healing and beliefs on the origin of illness as there are psychic/spiritual healers. But in spite of the varied beliefs, a consensus as developed among the more accomplished healers. This is their philosophy.

Man is composed of three bodies: the spiritual body, the astral body (the aura), and the physical body. An illness is the direct result of thoughts or actions that are contrary to the basic laws governing the universe on all levels of existence.

The spiritual body, which is perfect and therefore immune to disease, rejects the consequences of wrong thinking or wrong doing. The rejected negativity must find a nest in which to roost, and that is within the human aura. The negative influence works overtime in the aura—constantly probing until it can cause a reaction in the physical body. When the weakest point of the physical body is discovered, the negativity manifests itself in the form of an illness or a disease there.

THE CAUSE OF AN ILLNESS MUST BE REMOVED BEFORE THERE CAN BE A CURE

Many psychic healers claim they can cure any illness. I believe they can, but I don't believe they *do*. If it is true that an illness is caused by wrong action, common sense dictates that the illness cannot be cured until its cause (wrong action) is removed. For example, if I have heart trouble because of cigarette smoking, my heart cannot be healed until the cause (cigarette smoking) has been removed. Still, if there is no cure, it does not mean there can be no relief for the person who suffers from an illness.

I have witnessed many cases of relief without a cure. One of the most memorable cases concerned a man who was dying from lung cancer. He was given but a few days to live, and the large doses of morphine no longer killed his pain. A healer was called to the patient's bedside as a last resort.

The healer visited the gentleman at the hospital.

Within fifteen minutes all pain had left him. The doctors attributed the relief of pain to "one of those things." The healer visited the man every other day. At the end of two weeks the patient was alive, still painfree, and asked to go home. And he did.

The man lived for several painfree months after his release from the hospital. And when he did die, it was a peaceful departure during his sleep.

WHAT ABOUT INSTANTANEOUS HEALING?

There are verified cases of instantaneous healing, but, in all cases I am familiar with, two common ingredients were present. One, the cause of the illness had been removed; and two, the "point of no return" had not been crossed.

WHAT ABOUT INHERITED DISEASES?

Andrew Jackson Davis was a nineteenth-century American prophet who spoke widely on the subject of inherited disease. "The Poughkeepsie Seer," as he was commonly called, claimed that a peaceful and harmonious mother was incapable of passing an illness to the unborn fetus. His claim that inherited disease is the direct result of the mother's own disharmony seems to gain credence as genetic research continues.

Many physicians today (mostly in Europe) counsel prospective mothers with known genetic problems to avoid pregnancy until they can achieve a harmonious state of mind for at least five days before conception. After conception, they prescribe three months without emotional stress.

CHILDREN WHO ARE BORN WITH DISEASES

Children born with a disease are born with the disease of the parent ("The sins of the father shall pass unto the children"?).